MARKETING MINDSET IN MOTION

Praise

"This is a fantastic book. Well done and very different from what's out there. An absolutely fascinating read. Leora takes you into her classroom, dissecting and learning marketing principles right alongside her students in a way that's not been captured before. You'll dive into real-world examples through their eyes and interpretations and, as a result, escape the often far- too-lofty and far-too-conceptual jargon that is most marketing books. I found that once I started, I could not put this book down. I learned a tremendous amount by viewing marketing through an alternate lens."

—Jim Joseph, Global Head of Brand Impact at FleishmanHillard, Adjunct Instructor at NYU, Author of *The Conscious Marketer*

"An engaging guidebook that proves hospitality is the competitive advantage. Full of real-world examples and practical takeaways you can use right away."

—Peter Yesawich, Chairman at Yesawich Holding, LLC, Founding Partner of YPB&R, Former Vice Chairman of MMGY Global

"A truly brilliant book—smart, practical, and full of heart, just like its author. It brings hospitality to life, not just as an industry but as a mindset, a way of thinking—for creating moments and meaningful connections. Leora reminds us that great marketing isn't about the loudest voice but about the deepest connection.

"The book's tone is generous, warm, and never preachy, which makes it so compelling. I felt like I was in a really good class or a comfortable late-night conversation. This book is generous and useful while also full of soul. I'm so excited for everyone who will learn from this book."

—Patti Brown, Associate Dean MBA and Executive Degree Programs, Saïd Business School, University of Oxford

"I LOVED this book!

"*Marketing Mindset in Motion* is a powerful guide for anyone in professional services who wants to elevate how they connect with clients. Leora makes a powerful case that hospitality is more than an industry; it's a mindset rooted in personalization, care, and anticipation that creates real competitive advantage. For B2B services firms, this reinforces that client loyalty doesn't come from transactions alone, but from experiences that make people feel seen, valued, and understood. I found the reminder that hospitality-driven marketing builds trust and advocacy just as relevant in consulting as it is in hotels or restaurants.

"Equally impactful is the book's emphasis on research-driven insights. The examples of uncovering hidden challenges demonstrate how asking better questions leads to a sharper strategy and left me thinking about where I need to dig deeper. Combined with fresh frameworks, like the 'pinball machine' funnel and the insistence on aligning internal communications with external brand expression, this book delivers a toolkit for marketers who want to build stronger, more authentic client relationships. I left with ideas I can apply immediately."

—Suzanne Jacob, Chief Marketing Officer at DHR Global (talent advisory firm)

"Leora's marketing book is one that speaks the language of hospitality. This is more than a guide; it is a tribute to the power of empathy in business. With warmth, wisdom, and deep industry insight, *Marketing Mindset in Motion* motivates us to lead with heart, think with purpose, and serve with intention."

—Abe Monzon, Vice President of Talent and Development at Union Square Hospitality Group

Marketing Mindset in Motion: Inspired by Hospitality engages readers with easy-to-understand marketing concepts and real-world hospitality and tourism examples, showcasing how critical the experience and the emotional connection are for successful hospitality marketing. I especially appreciated the thoughtful attention to subjects impacting hospitality today—wellness, sustainability, and social impact—and how they're seamlessly woven into each chapter. And the chapter takeaways and reflective questions are invaluable tools for anyone serious about understanding and applying strategic marketing and branding principles. For those passionate about hospitality, it's a comprehensive and relatable guide that speaks to students, professionals, and executives alike."

—Julie Freeman, Executive Vice President,
Public Relations at MMGY Global

"Wow! Had Leora's book been around thirty years ago, my life would have been so much easier. This is a true marketer's guide to everything you need to consider and know. Reading this book is like going to school and working in the industry for years and years. Regardless of the experience level, Leora takes owners, operators, and marketing executives on an in-depth journey into the world of hospitality marketing. While the book is brimming with practical and technical applications, Leora's storytelling style makes the reader's journey very user-friendly and fun, too! Trust me, grab this book before you make any of your next moves. Your hotel and/or restaurant will have an insider's guide that will ensure it becomes a huge success!"

—Andrew Freeman, CEO/President of af&co,
Co-Founder of Carbonate Group

"It's great. What I loved most about *Marketing Mindset in Motion* is how fresh and usable it is. Leora takes marketing frameworks we all know and makes them practical with hospitality-driven insights, real-world examples, and scorecards that guide you step by step. The section on conscious marketing and partnerships especially stood out to me; it is a timely, relevant, and powerful reminder that values are what build trust and loyalty. This book isn't just another marketing guide; it's a smart, strategic, and inspiring playbook you'll want to put into action."

—Emily Goldfischer, Founder of hertelier and Former
Vice President of Public Relations
at Loews Hotels

"I really enjoyed this read. Each chapter offers detailed information, pitfalls to avoid, and real-world examples to bring the content to life. Marketing mantras are called out, score cards are provided to track your progress, and easy-to-access lists of strategic next steps are shared that are applicable to your unique challenges or opportunities. I can see this used as a quick reference on bookshelves across corporate America."

—Lorie Juliano, Global Head of
Communication at Sonesta

"This just might be the ultimate guide to not only understanding and speaking the language of marketing but also successfully applying it to your life and your business. Building upon her *Marketing Mindset* mantras and philosophies, Leora provides a thoughtful, clear, and precise approach to thinking about marketing and communication that can benefit everyone from novice to seasoned professional. Touching upon virtually every aspect of the marketing toolkit, this book is destined to become a must-read for anyone confronting the complex challenges of today's marketplace."

—Gary Leopold, Former Chairman and President of marketing firm ISM and President of the MAGNET Global Agency Network

"The book is a fantastic, practical how-to for anyone in the early stages of their marketing career, but it's also a great reference book for those of us in the industry for a long time. It's so easy to forget some of the critical foundational ideas, and I think it is something people should go back to a few times each year as a reminder or share with their teams.

"I love how it blends theory with real-world application. It gives you easy-to-understand and easy-to-execute theories that you can start applying the very next day. And Leora blends the heart and the head in her commentary. It's not just about bottom-line results. It's also about how you make your customers feel and the impact you make with your marketing efforts that matters. Love that.

—JoAnne Borselli, Group Brand Director at Connelly Partners

"For seasoned professionals outside the hospitality space, this book offers a refreshing perspective—one that replaces the usual CPG and HBR examples with real-world scenarios unique to tourism. It's a great way to reframe your approach to marketing challenges through a new and dynamic lens. I've already started using key takeaways to inspire my LinkedIn posts and spark my thought-leadership content.

"For those new to hospitality marketing or transitioning into tourism from another field, Leora provides a practical, accessible roadmap for applying core marketing principles in this sector. I plan to recommend it to every new member of my tourism marketing agency.

"Whether you're a veteran or just starting out, you'll come away with new insights you can put into practice—and a renewed confidence in the strategic thinkers shaping the future of our field."

—Karyl Leigh Barnes, President of Development Counsellors International

"Kudos to Leora for putting a spotlight on the principles of hospitality—anticipation, personalization, exceptional service, innovative and memorable experiences—and reminding us that they are vital components for any business aiming to connect with its audience. So many lessons learned from this book. I have truly adjusted my marketing mindset!"

—Laura Davidson, CEO and Founder of LDPR

"*Marketing Mindset in Motion* reminds us that the best marketing isn't loud; it's thoughtful, strategic, and grounded in hospitality. As someone who builds campaigns every day, I found this book packed with real-world value. It's the kind of marketing guide you'll want to keep on your desk."

—Todd Philie, CMO
at Southcoast Marketing Group

"It's fantastic. Leora's expertise shines through every page, turning necessary concepts into clear and actionable lessons. I absolutely recommend this book, which stands out for its emphasis on human connection. Leora reminds us that beyond tools and strategies, relationships are at the core of any impactful communication. This perspective makes the book deeply valuable. By combining theory with lived experience, Leora has created a work that is essential."

—Florine Cagnat, Founder of Dix Louvois Paris,
Global PR and Digital Communications

"Superb book! Leora's book *Marketing Mindset in Motion* is a natural follow-up to *Developing Your Marketing Mindset*, though it certainly stands on its own. The book is full of practical applications. It does not read like an 'academic' piece; it is for practitioners. I really like the analogy of marketing to hospitality, for example, anticipating the needs of different consumers on different occasions—a theme that permeates this book. Really well done. Highly recommend."

—Dave Roberts, Faculty at Nolan School of Hotel Administration, SC Johnson College of Business, Cornell University

"This book is a real point of reference for anyone approaching marketing. Its easy-to-read narrative is supported by real-life anecdotes and case studies, allowing the reader to fully understand the concepts and their practical application in creating a marketing plan. Leora's professional expertise provides an insider's look at the emotional marketing approach of the hospitality industry, and every page of the book can be directly applied in a much wider marketing arena. This is a pleasure to read and a very useful book for anyone willing to develop professional marketing skills."

—Marco Ferrari, Owner of Marco Ferrari Branding

"I truly love this book. Leora's passion for hospitality, teaching, and marketing shines through on every page. Her tone is warm, honest, and inspiring; she writes as if she's speaking directly to the reader. There's a wonderful energy throughout, making the lessons feel vivid and alive."

—Vera Manoukian, Former Senior Executive with Starwood, Hilton, and Sonesta Hotels

"Honestly, I loved it. This book made me pause, reflect, and reframe how I approach marketing. The book shares a standout voice for us to hear."

—Amy Silva-Magalhaes, Chief Operating Officer at Ultimate Care Assisted Living Management

"It's rare that a marketing book is both deeply insightful and genuinely enjoyable. Leora delivers an inspiring blend of storytelling and strategy, offering advanced marketing concepts in a format that's easy to read, easy to apply, and impossible to ignore.

"Whether you're a small business owner, agency strategist, corporate executive, entrepreneur, investor, or student, *Marketing Mindset in Motion* meets you where you are. It's a mentor, a blueprint, and a competitive advantage.

"Leora's writing is infused with energy, clarity, and a deep understanding of what works in the real world. Her stories, drawn from high-stakes hospitality campaigns and cross-industry collaborations, are vivid, relatable, and packed with actionable takeaways. You'll find yourself nodding, laughing, and, most importantly, learning."

—David Atkins, Principal at Digital DNA Infusion, LLC

MARKETING MINDSET IN MOTION

INSPIRED BY HOSPITALITY

Leora Halpern Lanz

ISBN: 979-8-89079-409-3 (paperback)
ISBN: 979-8-89079-410-9 (ebook)

Hospitality Strategies Press

Table of Contents

Foreword

When Leora asked me to write the foreword for this, her second book, *Marketing Mindset in Motion: Inspired by Hospitality*, my immediate thought was: "What an honor! But how on earth am I going to do justice to someone I've known, admired, and adored for many, many years?" My second thought was: "Of course I'll do it! If there's anyone who embodies the marketing mindset, in motion or otherwise, it's Leora."

Leora and I go back to the early days of our careers (we've aged beautifully if I do say so myself), when hospitality was glamorous and had a wonderful allure. Our respective and crisscrossing careers before Instagram feeds, influencer trips, and TikTok trends determined the fate of a restaurant or hotel. We were two young Jewish kids (one from New Jersey and one from Queens then Long Island) who landed in New York City with incredible work ethics. We worked hard and played harder, and we loved it. Here's how we met: back then, the marketing magic and ideation happened in boardrooms, kitchens, dining rooms, and yes, sometimes in hotel suites (hey, keep it clean here) or in the lobbies of the Sheraton New York Hotel & Towers and the St. Regis -- where Leora found herself hosting Paul Newman as he launched his salad dressing line, and then I took it from there to host the event itself at my place of work at the time, The Rainbow Room. Let me repeat that: Paul Newman, blue-eyed legend, movie star, philanthropist, with a salad dressing bottle in hand. It was the kind of moment only hospitality could deliver, and for us to work on that together was sheer joy. We tested our marketing instincts, developed the logistics of the events, and shared the excitement with those around us, including the local and national media.

Following the success of that event, Leora and I knew we were meant to be connected for life. There was our legendary trip to Los Angeles -a press trip that turned into a star-struck Beverly Hills tour. Thanks to my boss and mentor at the time, the indefatigable Joe Baum, Leora and I actually sat and dined with Wolfgang Puck at Spago. Yes, that Wolfgang Puck. He treated us to his now infamous smoked salmon and cream cheese pizza that somehow manages to be both genius and slightly absurd. Naturally, we both ate it with total delight. We treasure this moment, and maybe we both glamorize or sensationalize it a bit, but it will forever be our shared crazy memory.

And of course, there was the massive travel agent convention that we also worked on together, when it came to

New York City. If you've ever been behind the curtain at one of those events, you know it's organized chaos: thousands of people for us to meet, with other New York City hospitality representatives, hoping to connect with people who booked global business into our city. Somehow, through all the nuttiness, Leora and I found ourselves laughing a lot. That's what made it bearable, and memorable. We both understood that hospitality wasn't just for the guests at those conventions; it was also how we treated each other and ourselves. Those moments cemented my belief that Leora and I had something special: the ability to keep a sense of humor while never losing sight of the bigger goals. We were driven by our creativity, our common love for winning and, of course, the friendship that got stronger with each event where we worked alongside one another.

Wait a minute. Did I mention Elizabeth Taylor? Yes, the violet-eyed actress of the silver screen, Elizabeth Taylor. One afternoon in Bel Air, Leora and I found ourselves in her home, surrounded by her Yorkies, racks of her legendary costumes, and photos of her with Michael Jackson. It felt surreal, as if we stumbled into a movie set. We were there because Leora's time at the preeminent St. Regis involved her working with personal assistants to the stars, and for several consecutive years, the hotel welcomed Elizabeth Taylor and her entourage who stayed in a group of premier suites. Of course we were starstruck, but as consummate professionals, we knew that behind the glamour, this was about relationships, trust, and service. Taking care of her assistants and entourage when they traveled to New York was not glamorous work, but Leora knew it mattered deeply. That's always been her gift: seeing the big picture while remembering the small details that make hospitality truly hospitable.

# # #

Now over 30 years have passed (I told you we look good) and our lives have taken different directions. I landed in San Francisco with Kimpton Hotels & Restaurants for 10 years and then started my own agencies and Leora as you know has become one of the most distinguished hospitality professors at Boston University. Our friendship has always been built on the balance of a shared love of creative storytelling, a knack for seeing both disasters and successes as case studies, and the ability to laugh (a lot) along the way. Trust me, we've seen plenty of both. We've watched hotels spend millions on glossy campaigns only to forget to train their staff to smile. We've seen restaurants chase every trend in the book and lose their soul in the process. And we've also seen brilliant concepts so smart and so authentic, that you knew they were destined for greatness. Joe Baum, one of our industry heroes and mentors, was one of those visionaries. His restaurants weren't just places to eat; they were experiences, layered with history, drama, and joy. I know Leora absorbed those lessons, just as I did. They still inform the way we both think about marketing today. It's never about selling; it's about creating moments that linger.

What I love about Leora's work, and what you'll see on every page of this book, is that she brings both the heart and the mind to the table. Her "marketing mindset" isn't just a catchy phrase. It's a way of living, observing, and connecting. She has the uncanny ability to take decades of experience (ours, our mentors', and her own hard-earned wisdom) and translate it into practical, actionable insights. When I wrote a praise blurb for this book, I said, "Wow! Had Leora's book been around 30 years ago, my life would have been so much easier." I mean it. This book is like going back to school, working in the industry for decades, and getting a front-row seat to Leora's storytelling all at once.

The best part? It's fun. Leora can take a topic that might otherwise feel dry, like marketing plans, positioning statements, and KPIs or ROIs, and infuse it with real-world stories, humor, and humanity. Reading her words is like sitting next to her at a long dinner with a great bottle of wine; you'll learn a ton, you'll laugh, and you'll leave inspired to do better work. By the way, we recently had the chance to enjoy a long dinner (with a great bottle of wine) when I came to meet with clients in Boston and it was as if no time had passed. Ideas bubbled over and of course the laughs felt like a warm blanket on a chilly New England night.

And even after all these years, I still get to learn from her. When she invited me into her classes to speak with her students (even virtually) it was a full-circle moment. Here we were, two seasoned professionals who started out running around Manhattan trying to keep salad dressing launches and celebrity entourages on track, now sharing wisdom with the next generation of hospitality leaders. It made me realize something: friendships, like great brands, endure when they're built on authenticity, shared values, and trust.

So, to you, the reader: trust me on this. Whether you're a seasoned operator, a young entrepreneur, or someone just curious about the inner workings of marketing and communication, you're in the right hands. Leora will take you on a journey that's insightful, practical, and joyful, and she "always remembers the hospitality." She'll give you the tools you need to think strategically, act creatively, and stay nimble in an industry that never stops moving. How great that this book presents lessons that other industries can benefit from! All too often it's the business of hospitality that has to learn from others. But through this book, it's the EQ of hospitality that greatly benefits all industries. It's about time others learn from from our field.

And to this point, Leora reminds us throughout this book of something that she and I have always known and always believed: hospitality should never be an afterthought. It is the great differentiator. It's what makes one brand memorable while another fades into obscurity. It's what keeps people coming back, not just for a meal, or a hotel room, but for the way they felt in the moment.

My biggest question now is — who will play us when this book is made into a movie? I have some ideas, but I will save those for my next dinner with Leora. Seriously, go grab this book, dive in and prepare to be educated and inspired.

—Andrew Freeman
CEO/President, af&co.
Co-Founder, Carbonate Group
San Francisco

Welcome to
Marketing Mindset in Motion:
Inspired by Hospitality

If you're here, you're likely a business owner, marketing or communications professional, industry leader, or simply someone who knows that good marketing doesn't just happen. It's built, tested, refined, and fueled by a mindset that never sits still.

My first book, *Developing Your Marketing Mindset: Real-World Lessons from Hospitality*, encouraged us to think like marketers: to see connections, ask better questions, and think critically and strategically. Regardless of our industry, we must always remember the power of hospitality and the importance of connecting with our diverse audiences through meaningful messages that authentically connect through customers' need for community, wellness, or sustainability. After all, when brands lead with purpose and communicate and *educate* clearly, customers respond with trust, loyalty, and even a willingness to pay more. Informed, intentional marketing that educates people about solutions—whether for well-being, community, or sustainability—builds stronger brand advocacy and, ultimately, drives profit. But you don't need to have read that first book to get the most out of this one. *Marketing Mindset in Motion* stands strong on its own and is ready to meet you exactly where you are.

This book picks up where our mindset begins and turns good thinking into smart doing. Here, we roll up our sleeves and get moving. We'll shift from "How should I think?" to "What exactly should I do next?" Together, we'll sharpen your marketing mindset with real skills and subtle shifts that make a real difference, such as balancing digital and physical presence and connecting what happens inside your business to how the world sees it outside.

You'll learn to spot the real problem, pick the right partners, ask sharper questions, and design strategies that resonate; hospitality reminds us that great marketing is about people feeling seen, heard, understood, and valued.

Consider this your backstage pass to frameworks, fresh examples, and practical tools you can actually use. From researching smarter to targeting better, budgeting wisely to blending digital and physical touchpoints that stick— this book is here to help you transform good intentions into real results.

So, settle in, grab your favorite pen for jotting down ideas, and get ready to put your marketing mindset in motion. Let's get to work.

From *Mindset* to *Motion:* The Next Step

If you've read *Developing Your Marketing Mindset: Real-World Lessons from Hospitality*, you already understand that great marketing is about more than flashy campaigns; it involves understanding your audience, crafting an intentional message, creating value-driven connections, and enticing the audience to take actions that move the needle and generate revenue or other desired outcomes. It requires your marketing mindset. To stand out among the clutter of noise and ads that perpetuate our senses, if our connections are meaningful and impact a guest's or the audience's emotion through purposeful and authentic elements of community engagement, wellness, or sustainability, then the marketing is meaningful. *This book* builds on those ideas and focuses on several important techniques for even stronger and impactful success.

If you haven't read the first book, don't worry; this book stands on its own. Whether you have experience in marketing or are just beginning to refine your approach, this book provides practical tools and case studies for guidance.

Why Hospitality?

My path to teaching hospitality marketing wasn't planned; it was a "happy accident." When I joined the faculty at Boston University's School of Hospitality Administration (BU SHA) in January 2015, I quickly discovered the joy of inspiring the next generation of passionate hospitality leaders and marketers. Teaching and mentoring students, alongside creating courses that connect them to real-world businesses, has been one of the most rewarding aspects of my career. The constant interaction with students, industry leaders, and my global network of colleagues keeps me learning, engaged, and always evolving.

Marketing and communications, especially in hospitality, require a deep understanding of human behavior, a commitment to innovation, and a strategic mindset. Over the years, I've developed and taught courses such as Digital Marketing Strategies and Experiential Marketing, where students work in real time with businesses to solve current challenges. Watching my students apply their learning, create a tangible impact, and graduate with a sense of pride in their work has been a driving force behind this book.

I draw upon the applied examples from the courses I've taught at BU to illustrate some of my key mantras for enhancing our marketing prowess. I extend my heartfelt gratitude to the hundreds of students I've had the privilege to teach, both in Boston and during my time as a visiting professor at the ESSEC Business School in France, whose problem-solving skills and enthusiasm for tackling marketing challenges have continually inspired me. Their joy in conducting research and devising operational and marketing solutions to our industry's intriguing and common challenges has provided invaluable lessons that are applicable across all businesses. I am excited to share some of these insights throughout the pages of this book.

(Just a quick note: The marketing strategies shared by our students were developed as part of academic projects. While some have ultimately been put into practice, the ideas in this book are intended as thoughtful suggestions, not officially linked to the companies mentioned. That said, our class has a strong track record; many of our students' insights have been embraced by the hospitality organizations involved in our coursework.)

Hospitality is the perfect classroom for marketing because it's rooted in creating exceptional experiences. Unlike industries that sell static products, hospitality is about crafting moments; each interaction shapes brand perception, builds loyalty, and ultimately drives business success. The lessons learned here are universal. Whether you work in hotels, restaurants, destination management, retail, tech, or any other sector, the principles of hospitality marketing—understanding your audience, anticipating needs, and delivering memorable experiences—apply across the board.

Inspired by my students' work and the dynamic challenges of our industry, I wanted to capture these lessons and insights in a practical guide. My goal is to help you *apply* marketing strategies effectively—whether you're an experienced professional refining your approach or a business leader looking to enhance your company's marketing mindset. The principles in this book will help you think more strategically, act more intentionally, and create marketing that truly resonates and impacts.

In hospitality, we often refer to our patrons as guests; however, throughout this book, I may use the word "guest" and "customer" interchangeably. Please keep in mind that your customer might be a resident, member, donor, or diner, and you should feel free to substitute guest or customer with the appropriate term for your specific service business.

This Book

This book is structured to help us apply marketing effectively in any business setting. We'll explore:

- Assessing the marketing challenge and determining what research will help guide our decisions. How do we stay focused? Who should we speak with to learn more?
- Marketing internally before externally. Why should your employees be your first audience before you ever target external customers?

- The difference between physical and digital marketing. How do we balance online presence with real-world interactions?

- Speaking the language of marketing and digital. How can we gain enough knowledge to navigate and leverage marketing strategies effectively, so we know enough to be dangerous?

- Knowing your audience. What messages can we craft to resonate and build brand loyalty?

- The power of the presentation. Why is our ability to communicate the message as important as the message itself?

- Conscious marketing. Why should we ensure our brand aligns with values and purpose, not just promotions?

- Reviewing end goals. What helps us measure success and adjust strategies based on results?

- Infusing hospitality into every interaction. Ensuring that warmth, care, and a service mindset are embedded in every communication and touchpoint in a service business is essential.

Hospitality as a Competitive Advantage

In a world where customers are bombarded with marketing messages, the brands that stand out aren't just the loudest; they're the ones that make people feel seen, heard, valued, and understood. This is the essence of hospitality. At its core, hospitality is more than an industry;

it's a mindset—one built on anticipation, personalization, and genuine care for people. When businesses apply hospitality principles to their services and marketing, they shift from simply delivering a product to crafting an experience—one that builds deeper customer relationships, drives loyalty, generates revenue (or results), and creates a lasting competitive advantage.

Companies like Apple, Zappos, and Nordstrom have long understood that customer experience is their greatest differentiator, and their success stems from an approach rooted in hospitality. Whether in tech, healthcare, finance, or retail, brands that prioritize seamless interactions, authentic engagement, and intuitive service consistently outperform competitors. A hospitality-driven marketing mindset ensures that messaging is personalized, relevant, and engaging, rather than generic and transactional. It encourages brands to listen, adapt, and respond with empathy—key ingredients for building trust and turning one-time buyers into lifelong advocates.

Today, consumers expect more than just products or services. Therefore, applying the principles of hospitality to marketing is no longer just an option; it's a strategic necessity. This book explores how embracing a hospitality-driven marketing mindset—one that prioritizes the guest experience, meaningful connections, and customer-first thinking—can set brands apart, no matter the industry. Hospitality is a competitive advantage.

Mantras, Mindset, and Measurement

In each chapter, the marketing mantras serve as essential takeaways, distilling the key lessons into memorable phrases that readers can easily recall and apply. *Mindset in Motion* prompts invite readers to rethink their approach and apply new insights to their business challenges, encouraging a fresh perspective on marketing. The accompanying scorecard, found in segments throughout the chapters, is designed to track this evolution, ensuring that as we progress, we actively challenge our thinking and integrate the marketing mindset into our daily practices. Inspired by the principles of hospitality, these techniques remind us that if we don't adjust our perspectives, we risk stagnation, leaving our potential for growth untapped. By embracing this approach, we empower ourselves to move the needle and think differently about our marketing strategies.

Who Should Read This Book?

This book is for someone looking to move beyond marketing theory and into execution. If you're a business professional, business owner, or marketer seeking to refine your technical approach, this book provides actionable insights with empathy, hospitality, and purpose as marketing differentiators. If you're leading a team, this book will help you shape internal strategies to align with your brand's external messaging. If you're part of a team, I hope you find nuggets of practical ideas woven through these pages that help you elevate your thinking to become more critical and strategic in your approach.

If you have not had a formal marketing background yet but recognize the importance of strategic marketing in your work, this book will resonate. And if you've ever wondered, *"where do I start?"* or *"how do I know what's working?"* - this book is for you.

Putting Mindset into Motion

Marketing is an ongoing process that requires both creativity and strategy, insight and execution. In the chapters ahead, we'll take our hospitality and marketing mindset and elevate it further. Along the way, I'll share practical guidelines, real-world examples, and tools that we can immediately apply to elevate our marketing efforts. It's time to put our Marketing Mindset into motion. Let's get to work.

Introduction
Marketing Frameworks to Shape Strategy

Before We Dive In, a Friendly Heads-Up

Okay, let's get this out of the way: This next part might feel a bit *technical*. If marketing frameworks and strategy structures aren't your idea of light reading, I won't hold it against you if you want to skip ahead. Feel free to flip straight to Chapter One and jump right into the stories, examples, and relatable moments waiting there. However, if you're curious about the simple building blocks that help marketers connect the dots and foundational concepts, such as funnels, SWOTs, and all those handy acronyms, then please, let's plow through this together and stick around. I promise to keep it human, not stuffy. A little boost of critical and strategic thinking never hurt anyone. Your future marketing mindset will thank you! (I hope.) Ready? Take a deep breath, and let's peek behind the curtain.

Understanding Your Customer

Features vs. Benefits

My long-time friend Gary Leopold, one of the leading minds in hospitality and travel marketing, recently reminded me, "It always seemed that clients and owners were focused on promoting the amenities and features of services and products, but were not nearly as skilled at connecting and communicating the benefits of those features. We must remember, consumers buy the benefits."

As marketers, we often remind ourselves, "It's not about what you're trying to sell; it's about what consumers are looking to buy."

Understanding how to connect and communicate the *benefit* behind a feature is critically important. Linking your product or brand to benefits and emotions—and, as I stressed in my earlier book, surfacing a more personalized, meaningful message by connecting a service or product to an individual's wellness, the environment's sustainability, or the enhancement of community—demonstrates trust, reliability, flexibility, value, and even fun, convenience, safety, and security. These are benefits.

Think about your business. Rather than listing a simple two-column chart of pros and cons, write a two-column list of features *and* their benefits. Then, connect those benefits to wellness, sustainability, or community—because you *can*. Just think critically and strategically, and you'll discover a more meaningful marketing message.

Before we delve into the more hands-on, story-driven chapters, we'll spend a moment with some foundational marketing frameworks. This part of the book is more technical; it may not feel quite as engaging or relatable to real-world applications just yet. But stick with it, please. These simplified frameworks are here to help us build a solid structure for our thinking. They're not meant to be overwhelming or academic, just useful. And once we get past this groundwork, the tone of the chapters lightens, the examples are more frequent, and the practical tools are far more immediately applicable. However, first, we must build the base.

Let's start by looking at some of the core philosophies that structure effective marketing strategies; they will help shape our critical thinking skills for strong marketing know-how. Understanding concepts, such as what I call the "original marketing funnel" and its evolution to a "circular version," and the "pinball model," Porter's Five Forces, SWOT and PESTEL analyses, the four Ps and Cs of marketing, and the Net Promoter Score (NPS) system, is important for developing a comprehensive marketing mindset. With a bit of knowledge of these essential philosophies, we can begin to understand the nuances of strategy and marketing, and apply them to our ventures.

These definitions are just the tip of the iceberg. Think of them as a high-level (very high-level) introduction—enough to grasp the core concepts and see how they fit into the bigger picture.

The Original "Marketing Funnel"

It is common to hear marketers refer to "the funnel." At the heart of traditional marketing lies the concept of the marketing funnel, a model that has long served as a guiding framework for businesses aiming to convert potential customers into loyal patrons. Originally depicted as a linear progression, the funnel illustrates the journey from broad awareness to narrow conversion. This metaphor vividly illustrates that although numerous individuals may initially express interest at the "top of the funnel," only a small percentage will go on to make a purchase or engage meaningfully with the brand.

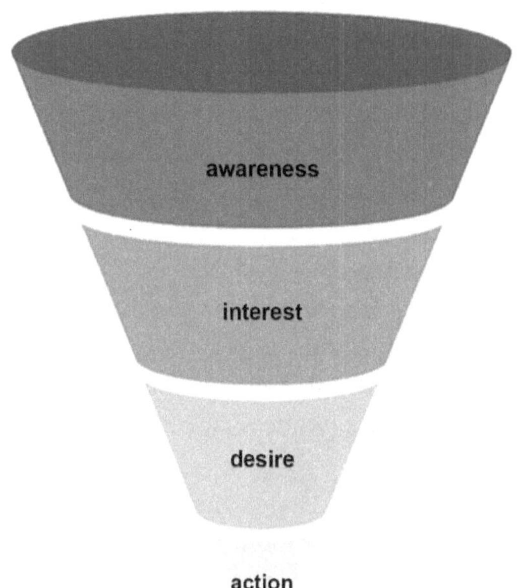

The traditional marketing funnel is typically divided into several key stages: awareness, interest, consideration and intent (desire), evaluation and purchase (action), or AIDA.

- At the top, *awareness* represents the first touch-point where potential customers become aware of a product or service.
- As they move to *interest* and *consideration*, prospects begin to seek more information, comparing options and evaluating their needs against what's available.
- *Intent* and *evaluation* reflect the decision-making process, where customers weigh their choices before finally reaching a *purchase* decision and action.

This structured approach allows marketers to strategize interventions at each stage to guide prospects smoothly toward conversion (action). However, there are limitations.

While the traditional funnel has been instrumental in shaping marketing strategies, its linear nature does not fully capture the complexities of today's consumer behavior. As customers, we have access to vast amounts of information and numerous touchpoints, so the path to purchase is not straightforward. The traditional linear funnel model neglects the significance of post-purchase engagement and the ongoing brand–customer relationship. This gap can result in missed opportunities to build loyalty and drive repeat business, which are crucial in highly competitive sectors.

The Tradition Funnel Evolved into The Circular Funnel

In response to these limitations, the marketing funnel has evolved into a more dynamic and continuous circular funnel model. This modern approach recognizes that the customer journey extends beyond the point of purchase, focusing on continued engagement and relationship-building. The circular funnel illustrates this by demonstrating how satisfied customers can become brand advocates, thereby fueling word-of-mouth referrals and repeat business that re-enter the marketing cycle. This cyclical process ensures that marketing efforts remain focused on acquisition as well as retention and loyalty.

The circular funnel retains the foundational stages of the traditional model:

- Awareness, interest, consideration, intent, evaluation, and purchase—and now also integrates additional layers focused on post-purchase experiences.
- *Retention* strategies aim to keep customers engaged through exceptional service, personalized communication, and value-added offerings. "Keep 'em coming back for more."

- *Advocacy* leverages satisfied customers to promote the brand organically, creating a self-sustaining cycle of growth. "Inspire your guests or customers to talk about you and do your marketing for you."

By viewing the funnel as a loop rather than a one-way path, marketers can implement strategies that nurture long-term relationships and continuously attract new prospects through existing customer networks—ideal for all service businesses, including, of course, hospitality.

Consider that hotels, restaurants, and other experience-driven, service-focused businesses thrive on repeat guests and positive reviews. By adopting a circular approach, these businesses can ensure that every interaction—from the initial booking to post-stay follow-ups—reinforces customer satisfaction and encourages loyalty. Personalized experiences and responsive feedback mechanisms become integral parts of the marketing strategy, turning guests into brand ambassadors who contribute to the ongoing success of the business.

But Today, the Funnel is a Pinball Machine. It's a Zigzag.

As my dear friend JoAnne Borselli, brand director at Boston-based firm Connelly Partners, was quick to point out, the circular funnel has taken a new shape. In today's reality, the customer journey is no longer linear nor circular. It's chaotic, unpredictable, and fueled by constant bursts of influence. Imagine a pinball machine: Customers bounce between discovery, research, delay, rediscovery, comparison, and peer input, all before they even consider purchasing—if they do at all. One moment, they're inspired by a social media post; the next, they're reading reviews, ignoring the product for weeks, then returning after seeing a retargeted ad or a friend's recommendation. Algorithms, influencers, ads, promotions, and real-life interactions all act as bumpers, redirecting attention and momentum in ways we can't fully map. Marketing today isn't about guiding a neat path; it's about being present and persuasive at every unpredictable turn.

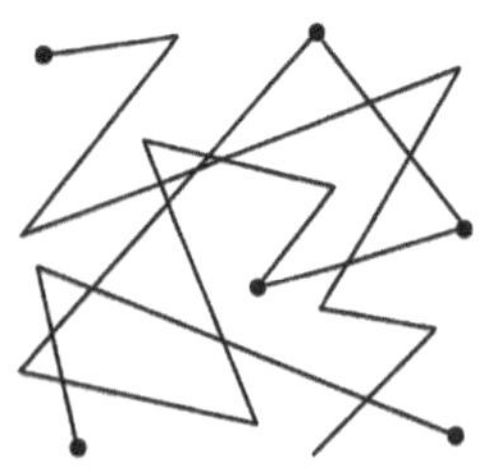

How does this help put our mindset into motion?
Transitioning from a traditional linear funnel to a circular model and now the pinball machine represents a meaningful shift in marketing strategy, especially for hospitality and other experience-driven industries. This approach encourages a holistic view of the customer lifecycle, where every stage matters and engagement continues well beyond the point of purchase. It calls for investing in tools like CRM (customer relationship management) systems and loyalty programs to support ongoing relationships, creating seamless, memorable experiences that both attract new guests and retain loyal ones.

Porter's Five Forces

Who is Michael Porter? What on earth are the Five Forces? Michael Porter is one of the most influential thinkers in modern business strategy. As a respected professor at Harvard Business School, he's shaped how companies compete, grow, and stay relevant. One of his most practical contributions is the Five Forces Framework, a tool that helps us see what makes an industry profitable—or not—and where the real competitive pressure comes from.

The Five Forces provide a reality check for marketers. They examine the key factors that influence whether a business can thrive or struggle. First shared in Porter's 1980 book *Competitive Strategy*, this framework is still used today because it works. Let's look at each force in simple terms and bring them to life with relatable hospitality examples.

1. *Threat of New Entrants*

   How easy is it for someone new to enter your market? If it's too easy, more competitors show up fast. But if there are big obstacles—like huge start-up costs, strong brand loyalty, or strict rules—it's harder for newcomers to break in. Marketers help keep those barriers strong by building loyal customers and offering unique experiences that new players can't copy overnight.

   For example, in a city with lots of hotels, a fancy boutique hotel might open its doors. To hold their ground, established hotels can double down on loyalty perks, special amenities, and local partnerships that make them tough to replace.

2. *Bargaining Power of Suppliers*

   Suppliers provide the resources a company needs to deliver its product or service. If only a few suppliers control something important—like rare ingredients or exclusive services—they can raise prices or limit supply. Marketers should stay aware of this force because costs and quality affect how you position and price what you offer.

   Consider the following: A gourmet restaurant depends on a handful of local farms for organic produce. If those farms raise prices or have a bad season, the restaurant feels it. That's why strong, fair partnerships with suppliers help protect costs and quality, keeping the brand's promise intact.

3. *Bargaining Power of Buyers*

   Buyers can push prices down or ask for more value if they have lots of choices or significant influence. When customers hold the power, companies need to find ways to keep them loyal and happy. Marketing helps by listening, adding thoughtful perks, and creating experiences that people don't want to lose.

   For example, if hotel guests keep asking for more, such as free breakfast or flexible checkout, rather than resist, a smart hotel leans in; they may offer new perks, strengthen loyalty programs, and turn price-sensitive guests into repeat visitors who feel valued.

4. *Threat of Substitutes*

   Substitutes are other products or services that solve the same problem in a different way. The easier it is to find a substitute, the harder it is to keep your customers. Marketers combat this by showing what makes their product unique and worth sticking with.

   Consider how traditional hotels now face competition from Airbnb and vacation rentals. To stay attractive, a hotel can offer meaningful extras like local tours, event access, or wellness amenities, so guests feel they're getting something they can't get elsewhere.

5. *Intensity of Rivalry*

> This is the competition among businesses already in the market. If rivalry is fierce, companies may lower prices or spend more on promotions just to keep their share. Marketers play a big role here by helping brands stand out in meaningful ways that make price less of a deciding factor.
>
> In a busy city packed with hotels, one might stand out by focusing on wellness and sustainability, offering healthy packages (please start calling these "experiences"), eco-friendly rooms, or partnerships with local wellness brands.

How does this help shift our mindset? Porter's Five Forces cultivates a marketing mindset by pushing us to look beyond our product or service and instead analyze the entire competitive landscape. Rather than focusing on quick sales tactics, we learn to anticipate barriers for new entrants, negotiate effectively with suppliers, gauge buyer power, stand out from substitutes, and strategize against existing rivals. This broader perspective ensures we are constantly thinking about how to position offerings, protect the brand's value, and adapt to market shifts.

Imagine a coastal destination that wants to attract more visitors. To do so, it must navigate competitive pressures all around it. This is where Porter's Five Forces come in. For example, the destination might face new eco-friendly island resorts opening nearby; this is the *threat of new entrants*, which means more options for travelers and more pressure to offer something unique. At the same time, the destination may rely on large, influential travel agencies or online booking platforms to bring in tourists; these act as *suppliers*, and their *bargaining power* can shape the destination's costs and profit margins.

By thinking through these forces, marketers can better see where pressure comes from and where to focus their efforts. Should they build stronger direct relationships with guests to reduce reliance on travel agencies? Should they highlight sustainability initiatives to compete with new eco-resorts?

Understanding these questions helps marketers sharpen their positioning. This naturally leads us to the next tool: the SWOT analysis. By pairing Porter's Five Forces with a SWOT, we can dig deeper to pinpoint what the destination does well, where it has room to grow, and how it can turn competitive pressures into opportunities to stand out.

SWOT Analysis

Yes, the SWOT is still a thing. For those who feel it's archaic, simple works, and this is a simple approach to assessing a situation. The SWOT analysis is a powerful tool marketers use to take a clear, honest look at where a business stands. It analyzes four key areas: strengths, weaknesses, opportunities, and threats. Think of it as a business health check: what's working well, where there's room for improvement, where new possibilities lie, and what outside challenges might be on the horizon.

- *Strengths* are the internal advantages that set a business apart. In the hotel world, this might be a strong brand reputation, a smooth reservation system, speedy check-ins, or beautifully updated rooms.

- *Weaknesses* are internal issues that can hold a business back—staffing shortages, outdated furniture, or a few less-than-stellar online reviews. These aren't failures; they're simply areas to improve.

- *Opportunities* arise from external factors or trends that a business can leverage. For example, if a competitor closes temporarily for renovations or a convention is coming to town, these can be chances to gain new customers.

- *Threats* are the external risks that could impact a business, such as new hotels entering the market, rising costs, or changes in travel patterns.

By looking carefully at each of these areas, businesses get a well-rounded picture of their environment. Highlighting strengths builds confidence, while identifying opportunities points to exciting growth possibilities. And calling out weaknesses and threats isn't about dwelling on problems; it's about spotting where to take proactive steps to strengthen and refine the brand.

For instance, in one of my marketing classes, we worked with a luxury hotel spa that offers just four treatment rooms. At first glance, that seemed a weakness compared to larger competitors. However, instead of seeing it as a setback, we flipped the narrative: The spa's small size made it exclusive and intimate—an experience only for those "in the know." What looked like a limitation became a unique selling point and a clever marketing opportunity.

How does this help shift our mindset? The SWOT analysis guides us to look both inward and outward, identifying our brand's unique strengths, recognizing and correcting shortcomings, scouting external opportunities, and bracing for external threats. Instead of simply broadcasting messages, we become more strategic, prioritizing assets that provide a competitive edge while proactively addressing vulnerabilities.

For a restaurant in a city teeming with eclectic dining options, for example, a SWOT analysis pinpoints what makes the menu and atmosphere uniquely appealing (strengths), highlights operational or service concerns to address (weaknesses), reveals new trends or segments to tap (opportunities), and flags emerging rivals in the ever-growing food scene (threats). With these insights in hand, our next framework, PESTEL, uncovers how broader external forces further shape the business's long-term success and marketing approach.

PESTEL Analysis

Oh, my goodness, there's more? Well, here's another paradigm to consider. The PESTEL analysis offers a valuable lens through which to view the broader external factors that impact a business. The acronym stands for political, economic, social, technological, environmental, and legal factors. By examining these areas, marketers gain a comprehensive understanding of the environment in which their business operates, allowing them to identify promising opportunities and anticipate potential challenges. Here's a closer look, with examples to bring each factor to life:

1. *Political Factors:* These include government policies, regulations, and the overall political climate that can impact business operations. Examples include tax laws, trade restrictions, labor regulations, or visa policies. For instance, if a country limits tourist visas from certain regions, marketers may shift their focus toward alternative markets or airlines without such restrictions to sustain visitor numbers.

2. *Economic Factors*: Economic conditions, such as growth rates, inflation, unemployment, and currency fluctuations, influence consumer spending power and market demand. For example, when the U.S. dollar strengthens against another currency, that destination often becomes more appealing to American travelers.

3. *Social Factors*: This dimension covers demographic trends, cultural attitudes, lifestyle shifts, and consumer behaviors. An aging population in Japan, for instance, may create demand for specialized services, while the widespread use of platforms like WeChat in China opens new avenues for targeted marketing.

4. *Technological Factors*: Advancements in technology can disrupt markets or create new opportunities. From digital marketing innovations to guest experience enhancements like mobile room keys and QR codes, staying current with technology trends is essential for maintaining a competitive edge.

5. *Environmental Factors*: These encompass ecological concerns, such as sustainability, climate change, and resource availability. Growing consumer interest in environmentally responsible practices and the impact of climate shifts—like Europe's increasingly hot summers influencing travel patterns—are key considerations for marketers today.

6. *Legal Factors*: This area involves laws and regulations related to employment, consumer protection, health and safety, and advertising standards. Compliance is crucial to avoid penalties and maintain reputation. For example, changes in regulations around short-term rentals in Paris and New York have affected lodging options and pricing strategies.

Conducting a thorough PESTEL analysis equips marketers with a clearer perspective on the external forces shaping their business landscape. This insight not only reveals potential growth areas, such as emerging markets or technological breakthroughs, but also highlights risks that require careful planning and mitigation. Ultimately, it's a foundational step toward crafting resilient, forward-thinking marketing strategies.

How does this help shift our mindset? The PESTEL analysis compels us to look beyond immediate customer needs or internal capabilities and focus on the *larger macro forces* that form market realities. This heightens our agility and ensures that marketing strategies stay relevant and future-focused rather than merely reactive.

As an example, for a cannabis dispensary focused on wellness in a newly legalized state, a PESTEL analysis highlights how evolving regulations (political), shifting consumer attitudes (social), and emerging technologies for product distribution (technological) open avenues for niche positioning, while factors like economic trends (economic) and sustainable packaging (environmental) can shape customer loyalty.

Do we need to use PESTEL, SWOT, *and* Porter's Five Forces as part of our understanding of the marketing challenge and the situation? In many cases, yes. While each tool addresses a different layer of analysis, together, they give us a comprehensive, multi-angle view. Using them in tandem helps ensure there are no major strategic blind spots, so our marketing plans are both well-informed and resilient.

- **Porter's Five Forces** zeroes in on *industry competition* and *power dynamics*.
- **SWOT** helps us balance *internal strengths and weaknesses* with *external opportunities and threats*.
- **PESTEL** scans *macro-environmental factors* that can shift entire industries.

The Four Ps and the Four Cs

This approach is one I easily share in the classroom. The concepts of the four Ps and the four Cs are also foundational in guiding the conversation around marketing. This concept is not about assessing the competition or the impactful macro scenarios, but about having us look at our business or service from the perspective of the customer.

The four Ps—product, price, place, and promotion—were first introduced by Jerome McCarthy in 1960 in his textbook, *Basic Marketing: A Managerial Approach*. McCarthy's paradigm provided a straightforward and comprehensive way for marketers to categorize and strategize their offerings. This model quickly gained traction and became a cornerstone in education, offering a clear viewpoint through which businesses could design, execute, and evaluate their efforts.

As marketing evolved, so did the perspectives on how to best approach it. In the 1990s, Bob Lauterborn introduced the concept of the four Cs in an *Advertising Age* article, challenging the traditional four Ps framework. The four Cs—customer, cost, convenience, and communication—shifted the focus from the product-centric view to a more customer-centric approach. Lauterborn's model emphasized understanding and meeting the needs and desires of the customer, considering the total cost to the consumer, making the product or service convenient to acquire, and ensuring effective communication rather than just promotion. This evolution reflects the growing recognition that successful marketing requires a deep understanding of the consumer's perspective and a commitment to creating value beyond the product itself.

As my college hospitality marketing professor, Peter Yesawich, recently reminded me, there's a fifth C that is critically important to remember. Competition is crucial from the customer's perspective because it drives businesses to offer better value, convenience, and communication. When a consumer incurs a cost, they want to find a product or service that not only solves their problem but is also easily accessible. Competition pushes companies to innovate, improve quality, and streamline access, ensuring that customers can find what they need quickly and efficiently. Businesses that compete well tend to engage more with consumers, establishing a sense of trust and reliability. Ultimately, competition gives customers more choices, making it easier for them to find their ideal solution.

If there is a fifth C, we also need the appropriate fifth P, which would be positioning. Positioning is about how we differentiate ourselves from the competition. But in the minds of our customers, the competition addresses where and how we stand out in their crowded marketplace.

So, for example, if I'm marketing a hotel, the product is the hotel experience, the price is the room rate, the place is where reservations are made (whether on the hotel's website or through an OTA [online travel agency, like Expedia]), and promotion involves broadcasting our message to attract bookings. This is a somewhat one-dimensional approach focused on reaching the masses. And in our course, we guide students toward the four Cs approach, which places the customer at the center of our strategy.

Perspective of the Business ------- **Perspective of the Customer**

PRODUCT	= **CUSTOMER SOLUTION**
PRICE	= **CUSTOMER COST**
PLACE	= **CONVENIENCE**
PROMOTION	= **COMMUNICATION**
POSITIONING	= **COMPETITION**

In practical terms, this approach asks us to reframe our marketing strategy to answer a key question: What does our product or service offer to solve the customer's problem? For example, if we're marketing a hat, the product isn't just an attractive accessory; it's a solution. Maybe it's the need for sun protection while still being stylish. Maybe it's simply the desire for an attention-getting accessory. By understanding this, we can better articulate its value to the customer, addressing their specific needs and concerns.

Similarly, the price must be considered in terms of what the customer perceives as their cost. Is the value offered worth the expenditure from their perspective? The place then becomes about ensuring convenience for the guest or customer, making the hat available both in physical stores and online, thereby increasing accessibility and convenience.

Promotion evolves from a one-way broadcast to a two-way dialogue or communication. Instead of simply shouting, "Here I am, book me now," we must engage meaningfully with our audience. For instance, seeing an influencer wearing a special article of clothing, a scarf, or another accessory on Instagram, coupled with targeted Google ads, represents a one-way promotional effort. But allowing potential customers to interact through online reviews or social media posts introduces a two-way communication channel. This interactive engagement helps build trust and fosters a more personalized connection.

Or, consider a hotel launching a new premium room category. From the perspective of the four Ps, the focus might be on the product itself: the upgraded features, square footage, or design. But viewed through the lens of the four Cs, we shift to the customer's needs *and* experience: What problem does this solve? Does it offer more comfort, privacy, or status? Is it a better solution for families, business travelers, or wellness seekers? This shift in thinking—from what we're offering to how it impacts the guest—often leads to stronger messaging, more relevant pricing, and more successful positioning.

How does this help shift our mindset? By applying the four Cs approach, we shift our focus from pushing our message to genuinely understanding and responding to customer needs. This customer-centric mindset enables us to refine our product, price, place, promotion, and positioning strategies, ensuring they resonate effectively with our target audiences.

Let's think about cruise lines for a moment. By shifting from the four Ps to a more customer-centric Cs approach, a cruise line can better align with what travelers truly want. This transition redefines product attributes into genuine solutions that reduce travel stress, addresses price as the total cost a traveler must consider, improves place by focusing on convenience, and replaces one-way promotions with dialogue-rich communication that builds trust and excitement.

For instance, rather than boasting about a ship's amenities, a cruise line might highlight how its all-in-one "package" (we will reword this as "experience" in a later chapter) solves vacation-planning hassles, or how straightforward pricing avoids nasty surprises. It streamlines booking by offering multiple departure ports and user-friendly apps, while turning promotion into an ongoing conversation, inviting previous travelers to share stories, photos, and authentic testimonials.

# # #

Having explored how to analyze our surroundings (PESTEL), our industry (Porter's Five Forces), our internal capabilities (SWOT), and understanding the perspectives of customers (Cs), we now turn to NPS, a metric that directly measures whether our efforts ultimately resonate with and delight the customer.

Net Promoter Score (NPS)

Okay, here's the simplified explanation of NPS and why this also works for marketers and organizations. NPS is a widely used metric that measures customer loyalty and satisfaction by assessing the "likelihood that customers will recommend a company's products or services to others." Developed by Fred Reichheld, Bain & Company, and Satmetrix in 2003, NPS has become a fundamental tool for businesses seeking to understand and enhance their customer relationships.

NPS is determined through a simple survey question: "On a scale of 0 to 10, how likely are you to recommend our company/product/service to a friend or colleague?" Based on their responses, customers are categorized into three groups:

Promoters (9–10): These are highly satisfied customers who are likely to actively recommend the company, driving positive word-of-mouth and contributing to business growth.

Passives (7–8): These customers are satisfied but not enthusiastic enough to promote the company. They are vulnerable to competitors' offerings.

Detractors (0–6): These are dissatisfied customers who may discourage others from using the company's products or services, potentially harming the business's reputation.

NPS is calculated by subtracting the percentage of detractors from the percentage of promoters. For example, if 50 percent of respondents are promoters and 20 percent are detractors, the NPS would be 30. The highest possible Net Promoter Score (NPS) a business can achieve is +100.

Achieving an NPS of +100 is an extremely rare and exceptional accomplishment. It signifies that every single customer not only had a positive experience but is also enthusiastic enough to actively promote the business to others. Hotels that get close to +100 can have a cult-like following due to extraordinary guest experiences, such as personalized service or exclusive amenities. Tell me where that is; I want to stay there!

Very few companies achieve a perfect +100 NPS due to the diverse nature of customer experiences and expectations. Most businesses have NPS scores that range between –100 and +100, with the average NPS varying significantly across industries. For context:

Scores Above 50: *Considered excellent, indicating a strong base of loyal and enthusiastic customers*

Scores Between 0 and 50: *Reflect good to average customer satisfaction and loyalty*

Scores Below 0: *Suggest that there are more detractors than promoters, highlighting the need for significant improvement*

NPS is easy to administer and understand, which keeps it accessible for businesses of all sizes to implement and interpret. Companies can compare their NPS against industry standards or competitors to gauge their performance and identify competitive advantages or gaps. By supplementing the primary NPS question with open-ended inquiries, businesses can gather qualitative feedback to understand the reasons behind customers' scores and address specific issues.

There is a hotel in Fort Lauderdale, Florida, that my family visited annually when my children were young. We really loved it there and enjoyed the amenities and location. But it was tired. It appeared that it hadn't been renovated for some time. It needed a refresh—more paint, updated fixtures, and new carpet. Each year, the hotel grew even more tired. Would we stay there again? Yes. Would I recommend it to someone else? No. I wouldn't want that friend to come back to me and say, "Were you kidding? This place needs a renovation!" But, for us, it worked. Now my NPS responses would be low. I'd stay there again. However, I couldn't recommend it to others. In hospitality, as in any business, word-of-mouth recommendations can make or break a property's reputation, thus NPS is especially crucial.

How does this help shift our mindset? NPS shifts our marketing mindset by centering our focus on the quality of the customer *experience* and the likelihood of recommendation, rather than transactional metrics such as sales. Instead of merely pushing product, we start asking, "Are we delighting customers enough for them to serve as advocates?" This shifts our perspective to long-term brand loyalty, encouraging continuous improvement based on direct feedback from promoters and constructive insights from detractors.

As an example, for global lodging brands such as Marriott, Accor, or Hilton (each with their own collection of over thirty sub-brands), tracking NPS pinpoints how likely guests are to recommend the chain to friends and colleagues -- which is an invaluable gauge of whether the brand's service, loyalty programs, and guest experiences truly stand out. By analyzing detractor feedback alongside promoter insights, these hotel groups can fine-tune their offerings, sharpen their competitive edge in a crowded hospitality market, and deliver the kind of guest satisfaction that fosters enduring loyalty. Research tells us that NPS correlates with business growth, customer retention, and revenue, serving as a valuable predictor of future performance.

Marketing Mantras

Whether we're examining the competitive landscape, assessing strengths and weaknesses, scanning the environment, or gauging loyalty, each framework equips us with insights for effective marketing. Here are some key takeaways from the insights just shared to help foster critical thinking and thorough due diligence:

1. **Embrace the Customer Journey and the Pinball Machine Energy:** Every interaction builds loyalty and fuels growth. Focus on attracting new customers while nurturing lasting relationships that transform satisfied patrons into passionate advocates. Picture the circular funnel—then imagine the ricocheting energy of a pinball machine, where engagement happens at multiple touchpoints. Staying present across these moments creates stronger, ongoing connections with our guests.

2. **Broaden Our View Beyond Just Products:** Utilizing Porter's Five Forces, SWOT, and

PESTEL teaches us to see the entire playing field, from competitive rivalries to macroeconomic shifts. We can reach decisions with full awareness of potential pressures and opportunities.

3. **Turn Weaknesses and Threats into Action:** Identifying vulnerabilities isn't about dwelling on negatives; it's about identifying opportunities for improvement, strengthening brand strategies, and staying competitive.

4. **Market the "Why," Not Just the "What:"** It's easy to get swept up in touting our product's features, but customers ultimately want to know *why* those features matter for *them*. Rather than listing technical specs or capabilities, speak to the deeper benefits, the problems solved, and the real-life improvements a customer can expect. This will connect on an emotional and practical level that resonates far more powerfully than a simple list of product attributes.

5. **Measure the Human Factor:** NPS reminds us that customers are people who can become vocal advocates or detractors.

The frameworks we've just reviewed provide us with essential tools to evaluate where we stand and where we might go. Knowing them is part of the equation; they give structure to our thinking and a foundation for what comes next. Now that we've taken a quick spin through these concepts, let's take a breath. The heavy lifting is behind us—for now. In the next chapter, we'll dive into the importance of assessing our situation and moving forward with primary and secondary research to gather the right insights leading to sharper, smarter marketing decisions. Ready? Let's roll.

Marketing Mindset in Motion

Great marketers don't guess; they use frameworks to decode challenges and shape strategy. Take a real or hypothetical business challenge and choose one framework—SWOT, Porter's Five Forces, PESTEL, or the circular funnel—to analyze it. What insights emerge? How does this shift your strategic approach?

1

Primary and Secondary Research for Smarter Marketing

If you skipped the Introduction, welcome to Chapter 1. If you just read through the marketing frameworks and need a minute to digest, take your time. When you are ready, this chapter will help boost the marketing mindset forward by exploring the question, "How do we begin?"

Effective marketing means understanding our target markets, and this understanding is driven by the quality of our research. Whether we're expanding target markets to capture new opportunities or narrowing the focus to a specific niche, knowing our audience is essential. To do this, we rely on primary and secondary information.

Primary research involves gathering new data directly from the source—conducting surveys, interviews, focus groups, or observations. It's firsthand information providing specific insights into our customers' behaviors, preferences, and needs. For example, we might survey our current customers to understand their satisfaction with products or services, or conduct focus groups to explore their reactions to a new product idea.

Secondary research, on the other hand, involves analyzing existing data collected by others. This would include market reports, industry statistics, academic studies, or even competitor analysis. Secondary research helps us understand broader market trends and benchmark our company against others in the industry.

Both types of research are crucial, and choosing the *right* research method depends on specific goals. For instance, if we're looking to understand a niche market, primary research can provide targeted information not available through secondary sources. Or if we're looking to understand broader industry trends, secondary research can provide a comprehensive overview.

Assessing the Situation: Stay True to the Challenge, Open to the Insights

Before diving into primary and secondary research, we must first pause to assess the situation: What is the marketing challenge? What problem are we, as marketers, tasked with solving? To start the process, we revisit the strategic frameworks for analysis shared in the introduction—the SWOT, PESTEL, digital presence audits, competitive sets, and more. These tools help frame the challenge, establish context, and direct our inquiry. Let's start there to begin learning and unearthing more context.

During this discovery phase, we often surface more than expected. Conversations with guests or customers, survey data, and environmental scanning can reveal new problems or opportunities that feel more urgent than the initial challenge. It's tempting to pivot. But in marketing, focus is power. When we stay grounded in the original brief, we create clarity—and paradoxically, we often resolve other issues in the process.

Here are three quick examples from among my many student consulting teams over the years that illustrate this principle:

- A collection of gyms throughout the city of Boston tasked a student team with promoting their new spas and telling a compelling story about "recovery and regeneration." The regional directors and the operations director wanted to inform and educate locals about the accessibility of injury recovery techniques at their spas. Through surveys with hospitality experts, local patrons, and deeper community outreach, the student team uncovered a bigger issue: Community members didn't even know these gyms had spas. The core challenge wasn't about messaging the benefits of spa recovery; it was about basic brand awareness. Still, by returning to the original goal—to attract new users—they found that leading with a powerful regeneration narrative *was* the right message to raise awareness, once the real obstacle had been revealed.

- The InterContinental Boston, an IHG Hotel, years ago, asked one of my student teams to develop a marketing campaign to help erase the stigma around hotel dining. Guests and locals were not dining in the hotel, but through first-person research, the students discovered the issue wasn't stigma. It was a complete lack of awareness. Most people interviewed simply didn't know the hotel had restaurants at all. With no exterior signage, no digital geotargeting, and no local marketing efforts, the property was missing basic "top of the funnel" awareness tools. The team shifted the focus to visibility tactics, proving once again that asking the right questions and staying engaged with the initial challenge helps uncover the truest path forward.

- A branded hotel in Boston's Back Bay asked our students to uncover why its guest satisfaction scores were not improving for its newly renovated and expanded gym. As the research progressed, the students learned that the entire brand was undergoing a larger repositioning and rebranding effort. Understandably, they questioned how gym strategy could matter amidst such broader changes. However, by staying true to the original challenge and focusing on the guest's wellness or workout experience, the students delivered gym-related recommendations that ultimately supported, and even elevated, the larger brand repositioning. The students showed the hotel's sales and executive teams that their gym marketing recommendations would remain effective, even if the company rebranded. This was a reminder that even focused marketing ideas can have an impact across an entire brand.

"How could our much smaller task of focusing on the gym satisfaction scores possibly matter in the grand scheme of an overall rebrand? We initially focused our research on the brand itself to understand the reasons they were considering a refresh and update. We learned a lot through our research and conversations, but at one point, we felt scattered and unsure where to even begin. We spent so much time focusing on the rebrand and were unsure how to approach our challenge. We had so many ideas, and they were so 'all over the place' that we realized we weren't strategic; we were collecting so much information and trying to accomplish too much with our marketing that we felt this was a futile exercise. That's when we were reminded to 'stay focused on the task at hand.'

"We regrouped and redirected to the initial challenge: increasing guest satisfaction for the hotel's newly renovated gym. We took a closer look at all the potential touchpoints we could use to communicate and enhance its value. As we did, we came to an important realization: Our deep dive into the brand, which had once felt like a distraction, had actually become one of our greatest strengths. It gave us a strong foundation and a clear sense of what both current and future guests would value.

"Ultimately, we understood that many of our recommendations could succeed regardless of whether the brand redefined itself. The key was focus. That clarity gave us direction and renewed confidence to move forward with purpose."

—Amanda Lohnes, BU School of Hospitality
Administration, Class of 2025

These simplified summaries of the projects we tackled in our semesters underscore the importance of outside eyes. When we're working *in* a situation for too long, it becomes hard to see the brand from an outsider's perspective—our customers' perspective. However, when we stay focused on the task at hand and conduct thoughtful, unbiased research, we solve more than just the stated problem; we build stronger, more relevant solutions overall.

Armed with Information

Knowing the situation and the marketing challenge we aim to address, we now need to collect data. Armed with information from research, we can develop innovative marketing recommendations. Here are a few notes to consider:

- At the heart of hospitality marketing is the ability to anticipate and meet guest needs. Through comprehensive research, including surveys, focus groups, review sites[1], and social media monitoring, we gain invaluable knowledge into guests' preferences, desires, and pain points. For instance, analyzing feedback from guest satisfaction surveys might reveal a growing demand for eco-friendly amenities, wellness services, or an increasing preference (or distaste) for contactless check-in options.

- It's crucial to understand the competitive landscape thoroughly. By conducting competitive analyses, we can identify gaps in the market, assess competitors' strengths and weaknesses, and pinpoint areas where we can differentiate ourselves. For example, analyzing competitor pricing strategies might motivate us to create and offer "experiences" (don't call it "packages," please) or value-adds appealing to price-conscious travelers. If a hotel owner is considering repositioning their restaurant and research shows competitors focus on fine dining, this opens the door for a more casual, experiential concept that draws a wider audience and increases visits.

- Effective marketing requires an understanding of the nuances of today's guests, travelers, diners, and customers. I encourage students to assess psychographics, behaviors, and preferences rather than just demographic segmentation. Why? Because today, age does not necessarily determine travel, hotel, or dining preferences—nor does income level. It's the desire and intention for the experience that determines the choice. It's their *mindset.* For example, if a luxury resort uses psychographic data to tailor marketing campaigns focused on adventure-seeking travelers rather than targeting by age group, this shift can potentially result in a significantly increased percentage of bookings from younger demographics who were drawn to the experience-driven messaging or older prospects who have the desire as well. Research helps us create curated experiences tailored to the psyche and mindset of the individual, not just age.

- Research and analysis enable us to identify emerging trends and adapt our marketing strategies accordingly. For example, analyzing social media trends might reveal a surge in interest in sustainable travel experiences, prompting us to highlight our eco-friendly initiatives in marketing campaigns. (Oh, and yes, we must market our sustainability initiatives, as shared in the first book of this companion set series.)

- By analyzing guest feedback from various touch-points, such as online reviews, customer service interactions, and post-stay surveys, we can identify areas for improvement and implement data-driven decisions to enhance the guest experience. For instance, analyzing common themes in negative reviews might highlight recurring issues with cleanliness, prompting us to invest in additional staff training or quality control measures.[2]

Research, Analyze, and Ask Questions

Student Memory: Former student and teaching assistant Paulina reflects on a fun restaurant concept and marketing project, and emphasizes the importance of staying curious and well-informed. We want to avoid presenting to a client only to discover they launched a new website that morning without our knowledge.

Reimagining Waterfront Dining: Using Research to Elevate the Sea Grille Experience

Student: Paulina Preciat

School: BU School of Hospitality Administration

Graduation: Class of 2023

The Marketing Challenge: The Boston Harbor Hotel at Rowes Wharf asked us to assist with re-concepting one of its restaurants, Sea Grille. As shared in the marketing plan's executive summary, "Sea Grille is a casual yet chic seafood spot with a waterside patio overlooking the Boston Harbor featuring a stunning view. Rowes Wharf Sea Grille offers inventive menus delivering the sea directly to your table. Chef David Daniels is an expert in preparing seafood dishes known for their quality and depth of flavor. He sources the freshest catches daily from local waters and cooks with seasonal ingredients." The marketing plan focused on enhancing the Sea Grille's experience with fresh perspectives from a clientele of Millennial mindset.[3] The objective was to bolster Sea Grille to become a "dining destination" and not just "a restaurant."

Outcome: SWOT analyses (strengths, weaknesses, opportunities, threats) and a PESTEL analysis of macro factors that impacted the business at the time (political, economic, societal, technological, environmental, and legal) were conducted. Primary and secondary research (mostly qualitative conversations with local and national experts in food and beverage trends and in "placemaking" [destination creation]) led the team to build Sea Grill "2.0" as a place to experience and to market it as a "bucket-list visit in Boston." Chef David participated in the final presentation and noted the elevation of the restaurant through this approach.

At the time, Sea Grille was the only restaurant at the hotel, featuring breakfast, lunch, dinner, and afternoon tea. Capitalizing on its vegan-friendly menu, "Instagram-able" imagery, and researching similar concepts in New York City, Los Angeles, Miami, and even Amalfi, the students created marketing recommendations that also included "employer branding," encouraging individuals to work there.

This student team recommended a new name for the restaurant (a bold and brave suggestion), so it projected a "sense of place." (They also explained that based on research, the suggested experiences and menu items strengthened the "localness" of ingredients and met the dietary demands among today's dining public.) The name suggested was *Anchor Point, Boston's Harborside Dining Destination*.

The team took it one step further and shared with Chef David that "each of our employees is also a consumer." Employee care is the primary value and mission of *Anchor Point* because if our employees are cared for like our guests, then our guests will feel valued, too. So, the team created a set of values by which to abide:

Values:

- Authenticity: Be sincere, honest, and upfront with staff and guests.

- Neighbor: Give back to the community; treat guests as if they were family.

- Commitment: Stick to our brand's values while being conscious of others.

- Honesty: Remain truthful to your ethics for the well-being of the community.

- Optimism: Think creatively, constantly evolve, and, most importantly, do not be afraid of a challenge.

- Relationship: Create a memorable experience for our guests and each other.

Can you see the ANCHOR in the values?

Paulina's Insight: "To stay current in the marketing world, read. Read books and articles every day. When we speak with clients, assumptions make us look unprofessional. We must read (the secondary research) to support the recommendations we have. We need the backup and the evidence. We cannot just make a claim.

"Another lesson learned: keep up to date on your client's social channels and website. I recall one of our teams suggested website recommendations for our client. The client had just updated their website a few days before. Fortunately, the team kept up and even checked the website the morning of their presentation, proving they were really on top of their research."

Did you catch this? It is critical to check the client's website, recent media coverage, and social sites periodically (and particularly the morning of your presentation!), so you can be as informed and current with your recommendations as possible. This is a great best practice. Keep reading to stay informed and armed with potentially useful information.

# # #

How do we begin our investigative efforts? Here are questions to guide marketers effectively through the research and due diligence process:

1. *Define the Target Market:* Do you have a clear definition of your target market? Are you expanding or narrowing it for the upcoming year? Who are your primary audiences, and how do you prioritize them? What specific needs or desires are you addressing for your target audiences? Can we describe the perfect customer experience throughout your organization?

2. *Understand the Brand:* What is our brand promise, and what differentiates it in a way that matters to your target audience? Are there existing brand guidelines we should follow? What key strengths, weaknesses, opportunities, and threats do we see for the brand?

3. *Analyze the Competition:* Who are our primary competitors, and how do they differ from your

brand in ways meaningful to your audience? What do competitors do well, and where do they fall short? Are there any comparable brands (not direct competitors) that we can learn from?

4. *Evaluate the Customer and Marketing Mix:* Is our current marketing mix delivering results? Assess the effectiveness of your channels, such as email, online ads, or social media. Which marketing tactics have been most effective, and which have not worked well? What are our primary marketing objectives, and how do we measure success? Is social media part of your marketing strategy? If so, do we have any analytics?

5. *Measure Visibility and Brand Exposure:* How visible are we in search engines, social media, and online ads? How will our market become aware of the business? How will our market trust us to have the answers?

6. *Collaborate with (Paid and Earned) Media and Other Brands:* What can we expect from our media partners? Do our partners understand the industry and help us reach the target audience? What brand partnerships or co-promotions have we tried, and were they effective? What brand partnerships do we need to create to achieve our strategy?

7. *Plan Timing and Frequency:* Are we reaching our target audience at the right time in their consideration process? How consistent is our marketing presence to stay top-of-mind?

8. *Assess Lead Quality:* How do we measure lead quality? Focus on programs that deliver detailed information, including contact details and areas of interest.

9. *Articulate the Overall Challenge and Strategy:* What actions have we taken so far to address the current challenge? How will we know if our recommendations have made a meaningful impact? What resource gaps and constraints do we need to overcome to achieve your strategy? What are the revenue sources we can tap to grow this business?

10. *Consider Miscellaneous Items: H*ave we conducted any prior market research? If yes, can we share the key findings? Do we have a reliable customer database? What internal communication tools or initiatives are in place to keep employees informed about marketing efforts?

Not every question will be relevant in every situation. Focus on questions that directly address the marketing challenge or opportunity. Tailor the questions based on the industry, market, and client context. Use the responses to identify gaps, strengths, and actionable insights that will inform your strategy.

The Right Research

Now, what does "the *right* research" mean? Here are a couple of examples to explain:

Prior to joining the faculty at Boston University, I led the global internal and external marketing efforts for hospitality consulting giant HVS. I also spearheaded the firm's marketing communications practice for the Americas and the Caribbean and managed numerous projects during my fifteen-year tenure with my dear friend from Sheraton days, Eydie Shapiro. When Eydie and I conducted due diligence of sales, marketing, and public relations challenges at various hotels around the country, we were often struck by how frequently company leaders wanted to implement changes without consulting their front-line teams—the very individuals who engage with customers daily. In many cases, simply asking questions of these customer-facing employees, or those directly involved in processes and product delivery, revealed practical, more effective solutions. My work today consistently highlights the value of respecting and leveraging the knowledge of those who are "boots on the ground," interacting with customers and understanding the intricacies of the business firsthand.

It's important to gather data and information from the right sources to make sound decisions, especially when those decisions are costly. In my first few years of teaching, I used the Darden Publishing case study "Euro Disney or Euro Disaster" to highlight the importance of conducting thorough and culturally sensitive market research. This case provides a compelling narrative showing that even a globally renowned brand can face challenges when entering a new market, particularly due to misinterpretations or a lack of appropriate research.

Lost in Translation: The Cost of Overlooking Local Insights at Euro Disney

When Disney expanded into Japan with the opening of Tokyo Disneyland in 1983, the company conducted thorough market research and developed a keen understanding of Japanese culture and consumer behavior. Partnering with the Oriental Land Company (OLC), which was deeply familiar with the local market, allowed Disney to adjust its offerings to Japanese preferences and create a culturally sensitive, immersive experience.

The park in Japan maintained the essence of Disney's American attractions while integrating elements that resonated with Japanese visitors. For example, Disney respected Japanese cultural norms and recognized the society's enthusiasm for American pop culture. This careful attention to local nuances, combined with OLC's guidance, contributed significantly to Tokyo Disneyland's overwhelming success.

On the other hand, Disney's entry into the French market with Euro Disney (now Disneyland Paris) in 1992 faced numerous challenges due to a misalignment between expectations and European realities. One key error was Disney's reliance on strategies that had worked in the U.S. and Japan, without adapting them sufficiently to the European context:

- Disney underestimated the societal differences between Americans, Japanese, and Europeans, particularly the French. Assuming uniform behavior across countries in Europe was presumptuous, especially since each nation has distinct cultural nuances.

- Backlash arose when Disney imposed a strict dress code for employees, clashing with the French culture's more relaxed, individualistic approach to dress. Even the American-style emphasis on enthusiastic hospitality felt insincere to many European visitors, who preferred a more understated approach.

- Disney misjudged European vacation habits, expecting visitors to stay for multiple days and spend heavily at the parks. In fact, Europeans preferred shorter, more frequent vacations, leading to lower-than-expected attendance and spending.

- French dining customs were also misaligned. Initial offerings focused on American-style fast food, overlooking the French preference for leisurely meals and quality cuisine. The absence of wine further alienated local visitors. Only after backlash did Disney adjust its menu to include more culturally appropriate options.

Over time, Disney adapted by offering more French-style dining options and relaxing rigid policies, gradually improving the park's reception and success. Disneyland Paris recently celebrated its thirtieth anniversary, and I had the privilege of bringing ten Boston University hospitality students to visit two of the park's hotels: Disney's Davy Crockett Ranch and the Disney Sequoia Lodge, thanks to Directrice Eva Gutierrez; thus, the changes made decades ago helped shape a new path forward.

I use this case to teach students that success in one market does not guarantee success in another. It underscores the necessity of modifying strategies based on accurate, context-specific research - it a crucial lesson in global business and marketing. The case also highlights the importance of asking the right questions and interpreting findings properly, especially when making significant, costly decisions involving brand building. Here's another in-class marketing case that shows why it's essential to understand the context, dig into the facts, and stay focused on the specific task at hand.

Winter Wonders: Promoting the Finger Lakes Wine Region in the Off-Season

Student: Owen Huzar

School: BU School of Hospitality Administration

Graduation: Class of 2016

The Marketing Challenge: The Tourism Board of the Finger Lakes Wine Region asked our students to develop marketing initiatives to persuade travelers to visit Upstate New York during the winter.

Outcome: In fall 2015, the student team recommended focusing efforts on three primary target markets—women's groups, young couples, and families. All were segments that the agency had already successfully engaged, and the team felt it was important to expand those three target markets. They were selected based on their interest in the activities offered, the market size, and the likelihood of converting website visitors into bookers of trips.

It was also recommended to geotarget and focus marketing on a three-hour drive radius of the region. While the agency had historically targeted audiences within a six-hour radius, the students suggested a shift to a smaller geographic (hyper segment/hyper local) area, enabling more concentrated and effective marketing and promotion closer to the region, with lighter outreach efforts beyond this core zone.

Owen's Insight: "This project prompted my team to conduct in-depth research of a wine region for which we had little knowledge. We asked what grew there? What styles of wine can be successful? What in the world is Ice Wine? The level of knowledge I needed to have about a place where I had never visited was daunting, especially when presenting to clients who lived there. We read, researched, and presented a plan for their winter marketing that had little to do with wine, but it strengthened our passion for the destination. We ultimately focused more on spa retreats, ice skating, nature walks, and fine dining. We also pitched the idea of 'hope for a new growing season.' So, while the wine research wasn't the 'right' research, we enjoyed what we learned and quickly pivoted to uncovering information more pertinent to our goal and intended recommendations."

Rediscover Revere: Strategic Branding for a Seaside City

Student: Micaela Yee

School: BU School of Hospitality Administration

Graduation: Class of 2023

The Marketing Challenge: The city of Revere, Massachusetts, sought fresh thinking to increase travel to this emerging residential and tourist destination.

Outcome: As part of the team's investigative work, there were three individuals who helped the students shape their recommendations and plan: An account manager at a Boston-based agency, which represented other comparable destinations around the United States, shared with us that "an effective tagline starts with a manifesto and identifying what the brand stands for." Additionally, she explained how influencer marketing is a very effective way to create a strong brand identity, particularly in a world where influencers constitute much of the social media space. The students also learned to drive more tourism traffic, specifically with overnight stays. Driving more traffic to the website was also crucial. Increased website traffic led to increased visitation and exposure.

A second important resource was a local real estate agent who enthusiastically shared insights into travel trends in Revere and who was able to describe the people historically coming to the city. The agent indicated Revere's property values had increased from 10 to 12 percent, attributed to the investment in the beach and infrastructure. "Travelers who come during September and October are mostly leisure [travelers]. Corporate travelers often go to Revere because room rates are cheaper than in downtown Boston. International visitors like to go to the first public beach in Revere and still feel comfortable in a multicultural city." This same agent suggested annual events such as Revere Day and the sand sculpting festival appealed to day-trippers.

The third extremely helpful primary source of insight was the principal of a highly regarded tourism marketing company, overseeing those operations and revenue management in the United States and Canada. Her best advice for promoting a suburban destination was to review the size of the marketing budget before deciding who to market to. "Once we determine who we want to target, it is then important to develop the marketing investment plan, which involves a combination of digital, word of mouth, and social media." Creating an overarching theme using a tagline was essential for us, too.

The students developed "Rediscover Revere," creating a theme around Revere's natural attractions. For instance, Revere can market its beach and nature trails as a unique selling point, given its proximity to Boston. The suggestions were shared in the structure of a three-phased actionable timeline, resulting in a hands-on, achievable set of recommendations, which the city of Revere began to implement within the following year.

Micaela's Insight: "Throughout this project, we were continually moved by thought-provoking questions and guidance to identify the right research and help us make decisions. This continuous charge to think inquisitively allowed each team member the freedom to explore quantitative and qualitative aspects of the location and many of its appealing features. This valuable guidance would ensure our solutions were practical, innovative, and well-researched.

"During the research phase, I often referred to a topic we touched upon in class—the significance of reading and staying relevant. By conducting timely research and eliminating unnecessary information, we were able to keep pace with current industry trends, better understand the landscape, and gain knowledge of the newest innovations in the market. A profound understanding of the market is essential for success. I also learned the importance of continuous inquiry. We were encouraged to ask critical questions, uncovering gaps in our research and enhancing our understanding of how to better address the challenge."

Disney's complex entry into the European market, the Finger Lakes winter tourism initiative, and Revere's branding campaign reiterate that conducting the right research is fundamental to smarter marketing decisions. The success of each project hinged on the ability to gather, interpret, and apply relevant data while avoiding the pitfalls of information overload or irrelevant insights. Disney's early missteps in France highlight the dangers of relying too heavily on assumptions or past successes without adapting strategies to local contexts. The Finger Lakes project highlights the importance of shifting focus when initial data, such as wine production insights, did not directly support the marketing goal. The Rediscover Revere initiative demonstrated how combining expert advice and local insights led to the creation of a practical, phased marketing plan that was both achievable and impactful.

One former student, Leonie Grundler, a graduate of BU's School of Hospitality and now CEO of her own board game company, explains how speaking with prospective customers helped her shift gears in the marketing of her product:

> People are often surprised when they hear my background is in hospitality. There are many subtle connections between hospitality and board games. I am still in the business of customer experience, bringing people together, fostering connection, and creating memories.
>
> The first time I presented the board game I designed, Biome, to the public at a large scale was at Essen Spiel, the world's largest board game convention hosted in Essen, Germany. This event is held every Fall, drawing 250,000+ board game fans from around the world. My stand at the convention reflected the game's strong nature theme and beautiful art, but what clearly drew the most attention were the tiny wooden chick and rabbit tokens, which are placed in small straw nests during gameplay. The number of comments from passersby on the nests and baby animals was astounding; it encouraged us to shift our perspective about the key selling point of the game, and therefore, it also shifted our marketing messages and strategy.

Conducting the right research involves asking the right questions of the right people, listening intently, and extracting actionable insights. Former student Annie Holcombe was compelled to share a similar story about the surprising and simple recommendations that surfaced simply by asking people the right questions. This is a situation that occurred recently in her work at a hospitality real estate consulting firm:

"We had the chance to work with the largest nursing home operator in California. Want to guess what often plays the biggest role in a family's decision to choose a particular facility for their loved one? The public restroom in the lobby—especially the women's restroom. Surprising, right? And yet, it's one of the easiest details to overlook.

"If you really think about it… who is the typical decision-maker or "shopper" of nursing homes for their loved ones? Typically, it is the daughter or a female relative. The female relative will want to use the restroom upon arrival. The restroom is the first touchpoint (in addition to the front desk clerkl). A restroom leaves the most important impression because it sets the tone for the rest of the site inspection. One more important point: most state inspectors are women, who also use the restroom when they arrive on-site. A clean restroom prepares the inspection for success and creates a strong first impression.

"It just goes to show that something that may otherwise be perceived as so minor or unimportant can have the most significant impact. We learn all these important factors by asking people. By researching."

Classroom Cases

Presented below are cases that highlight the essential role of integrating primary and secondary research in developing impactful marketing recommendations and strategies.

Sustainably Yours: A Two-Phased Campaign for Meet Boston

Student: Raegan Kelly

School: Boston University School of Hospitality Administration

Graduation: Class of 2024

The Marketing Project: Raegan and her team collaborated with Meet Boston, the destination marketing organization (DMO) for the city, to attract leisure, business, and convention visitors. This team's challenge was to instill a sense of "responsibility" among Boston area residents, visitors, and Meet Boston hospitality business members "to make meaningful changes with a sustainability-conscious mindset to preserve the planet for the future."

Outcome: With the platform provided by the Meet Boston team comes a responsibility to help champion the message of making the city a better place to live, work, and visit. Meet Boston can encourage its member businesses to participate in city-wide efforts, educate locals and travelers about sustainable tourism, and mitigate the city's rapidly increasing negative impacts of climate change and greenwashing (the act of making false or misleading statements about the environmental benefits of a product or practice).

The team presented a two-phased communications effort, targeting three personas, and used survey data and an incredible amount of qualitative conversational information with sustainability experts to understand the guidelines and parameters. The team spoke with destination marketers in Washington D.C., San Diego, Portland, Oregon, Victoria and Montreal, Canada, and even Italy to learn about the campaigns existing in other areas to dissect best practices. All this input helped develop recommendations for enhanced digital and physical presence with the message of promoting sustainable responsibility. The marketing suggestions focused on the sustainability of the people (the community), the place (Greater Boston), and the planet (encouraging locals and visitors to leave Boston better than they found it).

"Sustainably Yours, Boston" was modified to also connect with all of Boston's distinct neighborhoods, such as "Sustainably Yours, Allston," "Sustainably Yours, Roxbury," and "Sustainably Yours, North End." The slogan had the ability to work with corporate partners to help in this initiative, such as "Sustainably Yours, Levy's," for example, which also involved designing a "Sustainably Yours, Boston" certification.

Raegan's Insight: "It is easy to fall into the rabbit hole of jumping to ideas and conclusions. However, without evidence to support the creative ideas, the suggestions are meaningless. Through primary and secondary research, we developed a cohesive and detailed understanding of the target audiences as well as the entire ecosystem of stakeholders. The secondary research enabled us to notice trends, strengths, weaknesses, opportunities, and threats. This knowledge familiarized us with insights to anticipate, as well as what to avoid. We learned from the best practices (or failures) of others to ensure our approach avoided previous mistakes.

"The function of primary research is to fill in the gaps and provide the campaign with emotional attachments. It's crucial to understand behaviors, what target audiences enjoy, and why they make decisions. For example, through our group's primary research, we found 'easy accessibility' was a pain point for travelers to our destination. Additionally, there are numerous websites and platforms available for the guests of the city, but they do not know where to start. So, our team provided Meet Boston with the idea of implementing a mobile application, elevating the marketing and connection channels because it provided a solution for that specific challenge."

Time-Sensitive Lunchtime Service for Outlook Kitchen

Student: Mingjing He

School: Boston University School of Hospitality

Graduation: Class of 2019; ESSEC master's in data science

The Marketing Challenge: Outlook Kitchen at the Envoy Hotel asked us to market lunchtime business. Research revealed the need for a more "time-sensitive" lunch service to accommodate the neighborhood's working professionals and their limited mealtimes. This was also critical to competing with new entrants, such as Sweetgreen and Smoke Shop BBQ, which moved into the area.

Outcome: Suggestions included the utilization of Yext as a powerful tool to continually review the restaurant's digital presence and ensure consistency of information, such as hours, menu items on its site, and on Google, Facebook, and Yelp. Instagram paid posts were suggested, as well as neighborhood physical advertising on local Soofa boards (sidewalk electronic billboards) with dynamic and rotational imagery and messaging. Ads with a QR code enable audience interactions, further engagement, and the ability to book a reservation.

To attract the lunchtime business crowd, the student team recommended promoting the private dining room as a lunch meeting spot. They created a sample platter box and invitation card for the hotel's sales team to use during client visits, showcasing the concept. Primary market research revealed that most people had limited time for lunch, prompting the team to develop a to-go menu and partner with GrubHub. To reach into the catering market, they also suggested partnerships with Boston-based platforms ezCater and CaterCow, aiming to build corporate relationships through in-person visits supported by targeted catering collateral.

The students' survey research (fall 2018) revealed that many people who worked in the Seaport District dined out three to five times per week. Most people were willing to spend between $10–$16 on a quick meal, and some respondents indicated they would not spend more than $10 on lunch. (The second-highest segment of lunch-goers noted they typically spend $16–25 on lunch.) During the week, to-go lunch, quick lunch, and business lunch catered to their own distinct audiences in the market. Additionally, Google was selected as the most popular choice when respondents were asked how they search for a restaurant, followed by recommendations from coworkers and friends. Approximately 45 percent of the respondents reported Instagram as the platform they most frequently used. Among those who had heard of chef Tatiana Rosana, they either know her from the Food Network's show, *Chopped,* or from her personal Instagram account.

Mingjing's Insight: "To understand the lunchtime traffic for a specific hotel restaurant, my team conducted in-person surveys in the neighborhood, which was not an easy task at all. But the value of primary research far outweighs the challenge of obtaining it. At my work now, we also need to verify secondary research through first-hand investigation."

Modernizing Nuptials: Marketing Mandarin Oriental Weddings for a New Generation

Student: Leonie Grundler

School: BU School of Hospitality Administration

Graduation: Class of 2018

The Marketing Challenge: Although the Mandarin Oriental's success goes without saying, there is always room for improvement. In 2017, the hotel's busiest seasons were spring and fall, when corporate groups and business travel were flourishing. The hotel aimed to boost off-season traffic by hosting more social celebrations. Since 2016, the hotel tripled its social celebrations (mainly weddings) and still had the bandwidth in space and timing to double its number of social events. The Mandarin Oriental Boston sought to maintain its successful core values while introducing a new "millennial spin" to attract even more business.

The team was tasked with understanding how to position Mandarin Oriental in the minds of millennial brides considering Boston wedding venues. The students were asked, "What is the bride-to-be looking for? What stands out amongst the dozens of hotels in the city? How can the Mandarin Oriental be the place for the next bride's dream wedding?"

Outcome: The team studied wedding trends at that time and explored "what the modern couple looks like." The research led to a focus on couples with a "millennial mindset," who are identified not by age or income but by a strong desire for "personalization, breaking traditions, and making a difference." This mindset translated into numerous opportunities for Mandarin Oriental, Boston (MOB), including new target markets and various opportunities to present to potential wedding clients. The couples were reached through social media strategies, website optimization, and more. The traditional wedding cake had given way to dessert tables and exquisite flower arrangements. Research showed mothers-of-the-bride were the dominant decision makers in wedding planning, and there was a rising percentage of mixed-race or multi-cultural weddings, second weddings, and same-sex weddings. So, how does the hotel showcase imagery of prospective couples while incorporating popular and trending amenities and still maintaining its ultra-luxury brand value?

Leonie's Insight: "We personally interviewed professionals in luxury hotels and the wedding industry and gained insights from Pew Research Center, *Harvard Business Review* articles, and wedding industry publications, including *The Knot* and *Inside Weddings*. One of our primary sources, a sales coordinator at a luxury hotel in Boston, shared a valuable insight about the wedding venue selection process: 'Brand image plays a decisive role for luxury brides. They want to get married at a hotel that is instantly recognizable and unforgettable to their guests.'

"My key takeaway from conducting primary and secondary research for this project is that while primary research naturally offers a subjective perspective, it is essential for uncovering emerging trends directly from your target audience or experts who bring your research to life."

Late Nights and Live Music: Boosting Evening Patronage for BBQ

Student: Annie Holcombe

School: BU School of Hospitality Administration

Graduation: Class of 2017

The Marketing Challenge: Chef Andy Husbands is a local Boston legend as well as a Food Network national barbecue star. He is the award-winning chef, author, and "pitmaster" behind the Smoke Shop BBQ, Boston's acclaimed barbecue restaurants, and three-time winner of *Boston Magazine*'s "Best Barbecue," among other accolades. There are several Smoke Shop locations, including one in Cambridge's Kendall Square, the subject of this specific challenge.

Chef Andy indicated that he was keen to bring live music to the restaurant to help boost late-night patronage. So how do we market "late-night," and who is the customer? Is there anything we need to do differently to attract this new crowd?

Outcome: The team's primary research findings indicated women were the primary decision makers and planners for late-night activities. Women also emphasized the importance of having food, at the very least finger foods or appetizers, available so friends weren't just drinking at the bar. Food kept drinkers as diners and turned the evening into longer stays to enjoy the music. It then becomes "a night out."

Annie's Insight: "For our project, we wanted to explore the impact of live music and if there was even a desire for it from the market. We started with primary research to gain a better understanding of current trends for the live music sessions, which would be in place from 10:00 p.m. to 1:00 a.m. We conducted a survey through Facebook, targeting the intended demography of twenty-five to thirty-four-year-olds, to see what they would want or expect from a bar or restaurant music session. Of the seventy people we surveyed, 65 percent were between the ages of twenty-five and thirty-four. Though a small sample size, one of the significant trends we discovered was the importance of food during the live music sessions. About 88 percent of respondents said the availability of food was important in their decision to attend a live music gig. These were all extremely insightful pieces of information.

"A downside with this type of research? Due to the nature of the survey, which was brief and efficient for people to complete, most of the survey was multiple choice because we wanted to get as much participation as possible. However, this may have pigeonholed us with information specific to these questions solely. It's the secondary research that enabled us to discover another trend we would have missed: 75 percent of women make the dining-out decisions, making it important to have food and drinks appealing to women. This was crucial information for our project, and it helped us identify our target market."

Take Me to the Q: Lunchtime BBQ, That Is

Student: Parker Doyle

School: BU School of Hospitality Administration

Graduation: Class of 2019

The Marketing Challenge: When Chef Andy's Smoke Shop BBQ opened at Assembly Row in Somerville, Massachusetts, Partners HealthCare also opened nearby. How can we connect with the locals who live and work in the neighborhood to enjoy BBQ during lunchtime? The team determined that the initial challenge of strengthening the lunch business required a better understanding of the location in Somerville. The research involved observing the customer traffic flows, whether by foot, vehicle, or public transportation, which ultimately impacted the marketing recommendations.

Outcome: The information revealed by the primary research led the team to study a set of nearby competitive restaurants offering similar menu items. They examined the competitors and created recommendations for enhanced physical and online presence. With their overarching tagline, "Take Me to the Q" (barbe*cue)*, all signage or ads directed passers-by to the restaurant. Ads were to be placed on lamp posts and trains. Recommendations were made for "pop-up" carts and keywords for search engine optimization. A timeline was drawn to assist the Chef Andy with the smooth implementation of ideas.

Parker's Insight: "When evaluating opportunities for a business, research and talking directly with customers are essential. In my professional role, I have personally conducted over one thousand customer intercepts across various segments of the food and beverage industry, speaking one-on-one with customers to understand their perception of our client's business current situation and areas of opportunity.

"While quantitative research can have benefits, qualitative customer interviews allow us to thoroughly understand decision-motivators and business improvement opportunities. We can gain thoughts on new menu items, store designs, or logos. Qualitative conversations allow us to closely evaluate the customer's emotions; customer inputs often become the most critical rationale for recommended changes and cut through any corporate round-table discussion."

Building Community and Commitment: Strengthening Relations with a Thank You

Student: Maura Feltault

School: BU School of Hospitality Administration

Graduation: Class of 2017

The Marketing Challenge: The Massachusetts Convention Center Authority (MCCA) asked our student team to assist in communicating with the Boston lodging community. Our role was to help educate them about the positive impact of convention business in the city, with the goal of encouraging hotels to respond more quickly and to offer additional guest rooms when needed for conventions. The challenge was that the MCCA requires hotels to commit guestrooms years ahead of the conference, but hotels were less willing than in previous years to reserve many rooms so far in advance. The on-property salespeople reported to management companies, which reported to owners. The owners were not as comfortable committing to guestrooms eight, ten, or over twelve years in advance, because they could potentially command higher room rates.

Outcome: The most important outcome from the direct interviews with hotel salespeople revealed a critical opportunity. So simple, yet momentous. The students learned that hotel sales teams absolutely understood the significance of their cooperation and teamwork with the MCCA. The hoteliers told the students, "We just want the MCCA to say 'thank you' to us once in a while." The marketing recommendations immediately shifted to a communications plan. The plan included fun music or social events to invite the hotel teams and periodic news-letters with messages of appreciation and success stories. The MCCA implemented the communications plan and even invited me to attend. I filmed the first *Thank You* event and sent a video of the inaugural event to the entire class, all of whom had graduated the year prior.

Maura's Insight: "Working with real-world clients in our class pushed us to up our game and think critically. This was such an exciting opportunity for us to step out of the classroom and strategize. In every role I have had since college, my ability to ask the right questions and solve problems strategically, just as we did for those cli-ents, have always been immensely impactful."

# # #

Across the six case studies just shared, a common thread emerges: Successful marketing strategies are rooted in a deep understanding of consumer behavior, data-driven decision-making, and thoughtful execution. Each case illustrates the importance of aligning offerings with guest preferences, whether it's tailoring a late-night music experience to the right demographic, repositioning a hotel brand to match evolving traveler expectations, or refining digital marketing efforts for better ROI.

Due Diligence

This process of conducting due diligence begins with examining competitive and comparable sets to understand the industry landscape and benchmarks. It then extends to a thorough analysis of both the front and back end of the website, ensuring functionality and user experience align with strategic goals. Additionally, reviewing social media sites and evaluating their connectivity within the broader digital ecosystem provides insight into how well the brand engages with its audience across touchpoints. Together, these steps form a comprehensive approach to identifying opportunities and areas for improvement in the brand's digital and experiential presence, strengthening our marketing mindset.

SWOT and Comp Sets

A critical component of strategic planning in marketing is looking at the landscape through various lenses or frameworks. The SWOT analysis, reviewed in the preceding chapter, helps organizations identify their internal *strengths* and *weaknesses*, as well as external *opportunities* and *threats*. This framework provides a comprehensive view of a company's current standing and guides strategic decision-making by highlighting areas for growth and improvement.

The SWOT analysis must be thorough, honest, and objective. Weaknesses should identify areas where the company may be lacking, whether in terms of resources, capabilities, or market positioning. Opportunities and threats stem from external factors, such as market trends, economic conditions, and competitive landscape. It is helpful to experience the hotel, restaurant, product, or service to add even more intimate observations to the SWOT.

In addition to the SWOT analysis, understanding competitive sets (comp sets) is crucial for benchmarking and strategic planning. A competitive set includes direct competitors offering similar products or services in the same market. Analyzing competitors helps businesses gauge market standards, pricing strategies, and customer expectations. There could be a primary comp set for similar market segment hotels (luxury hotels within the Back Bay and Financial Districts of Boston), or there could be a comp set for hotels competing with our subject property for weddings, group business, or meeting space, for example. Perhaps it's a "secondary" comp set.

To deepen understanding and uncover additional opportunities, I encourage students to consider taking the analysis a step further, if time permits, by documenting a SWOT analysis for each of the competitors in the competitive set. While it doesn't need to be as comprehensive as the primary SWOT analysis, this exercise helps students identify key strengths, weaknesses, opportunities, and threats unique to each competitor. In this way, we can uncover gaps in the market, potential areas for differentiation, and untapped opportunities.

I also encourage consideration of what I refer to as a comparable set. These are businesses with similar operational models (and not direct competitors), including target demographics or service offerings. For instance, a luxury hotel in New York may consider a luxury hotel in London or Paris as part of its comparable set. By studying these businesses, companies can glean best practices and innovative ideas to adapt to their operations. This broader perspective can be valuable for identifying emerging trends and opportunities not yet apparent within our immediate competitive landscape. I remind students that when communicating these insights to clients, a balanced approach emphasizing strengths and opportunities while sensitively addressing weaknesses and threats is key to fostering a constructive and forward-looking dialogue.

While the examples above focus on hotels, these practices apply to any business because understanding the competitive landscape is crucial. Thoroughly analyzing competitors is an essential part of due diligence, helping businesses anticipate challenges, identify opportunities, and position themselves strategically in the market.

Website Analysis: Front-End and Back-End

The website is often the first point of contact between a business and potential customers. Therefore, evaluating the effectiveness of a website is a crucial part of our classroom lessons and strengthening our marketing mind. The website analysis involves assessing both the front-end and back-end, ensuring the site delivers a seamless and engaging user experience (UX) while also performing optimally behind the scenes.

The front-end of a website, which projects the user experience and the opportunity to engage with web visitors, plays a vital role in shaping their experience. Key elements to evaluate include (but are certainly not limited to):

1. **Navigability:** Try moving around the site. Is it easy? Does it work? The ease with which users can move around the site is paramount. An intuitive and well-organized navigation system helps visitors find information quickly, reducing bounce rates (visitors "bouncing" off the site) and increasing the likelihood of conversions (the action we desire—download the PDF, book the hotel room, make the restaurant or spa reservation).

2. **Working Links:** Did you click on any page links? Do they work? Can you get back to the main site easily? Broken links can frustrate users and harm the site's credibility.

3. **Photographs and Visuals:** Is the site attractive and eye-appealing with high-resolution photography and other visual or rich assets (video) to result in an engaging and attractive website? Photos should be optimized for fast loading times to prevent delays, which could deter users. These are among the roles of the web developer.

4. **Readability:** Is the language understandable? Is it easy to read? The clarity of text content, including font choice, size, and color contrast, affects how easily users can consume information.

5. **Calls to Action (CTAs):** No call to action on a site is a missed opportunity. What do we want the user to do? Book the reservation? Ask for more information? We must provide those CTAs in visible and convenient places for our web visitors.

6. **Mobile Speed and Clarity:** Websites are developed to be responsive, which means, in this context, it is functionally adaptable to all devices—mobile variations, tablet variations, and desktop, too. This includes fast loading times and easy-to-use navigation on smaller screens.

7. **Accessibility:** Does the website meet basic accessibility standards so all visitors, including those with disabilities, can use it easily? This includes alt text for images, clear headings, and compatibility with screen readers. An accessible site is good practice and demonstrates a commitment to serving all audiences.

8. **AI Enhancements:** Does the website utilize AI-driven tools to enhance the user experience or provide personalization? This could include chatbots for instant help, personalized recommendations, or dynamic content that adjusts based on the visitor's behavior. Smart use of AI can increase engagement and help turn visitors into loyal customers.

Each year, we see an increasing number of website visits and unique visitors coming from mobile devices compared to desktops. Recently, in a study comparing the differences between mobile and desktop users, SEMrush looked at metrics that define traffic: number of visits, number of unique visitors, average pages per visit, average visit duration, and the bounce rate (the average number of people who leave a page without any engagement). This doesn't necessarily prove a preference for mobile, but it shows the convenience of mobile devices, reflecting changes in user behavior, and the growing optimization of websites for mobile browsing. My point? If we don't test our websites on our phones and on others' phones, we haven't checked the usability of the mobile site.

The back-end analysis encompasses the technical elements supporting the website's functionality and performance. I am eternally grateful to my friend Todd Philie, founder and CEO of Southcoast Marketing Group, who visits my classroom each semester to show the students how his proprietary software can assess the "Google likeability" of a website.[4] This helps our students gain valuable insights into the back-end effectiveness of their clients' sites. Key areas assessed by the tool include (and again, are not limited to):

1. **Site Map:** Is there one? This is not something we would see from the front-end. A well-structured site map helps search engines index the website more effectively, improving SEO performance. It also aids users in understanding the overall structure of the site.

2. **ADA Compliance:** The Americans with Disabilities Act (ADA) Guidelines ensure that websites are accessible to all users, including those with disabilities, fulfilling both a legal requirement and an ethical responsibility. This involves alt text for images, keyboard navigability, and readable text for screen readers. Are there text sections that overlap with photography, making it difficult to read? Is the font so light that it's impossible to read? Or is the font too small?

3. **Compressed Images:** Image optimization is critical for reducing load times. Compressed images maintain quality while decreasing file sizes, leading to faster page loading and a better user experience.

4. **Speed of the Site:** Website speed is a crucial factor in user satisfaction and search engine ranking. Slow-loading pages can lead to higher bounce rates and lower conversion rates.

5. **Backlinks:** High-quality backlinks from reputable sites contribute to the website's authority and improve its search engine rankings. The more backlinks to credible sites, the stronger the legitimacy of the website, which helps boost its presence in Google searches.

6. **Widgets for Social Media:** Integrating social media widgets enables users to connect with their preferred social sites, allowing them to engage with the brand or product more regularly. Do you see the hotel's Facebook or Instagram link on the website so you can click and then follow?

7. **Social Shopping Links:** More brands now make it possible to buy directly from social media posts or through an influencer's unique link. This seamless connection between inspiration and purchase shortens the customer journey—so it's smart to check whether your website and social channels are designed to support this. Can visitors easily click from an Instagram post to book a room, buy a gift card, or make a reservation?

We have had so much fun in class over the years assessing the efficacy of our client websites. Is the URL in the search bar fitting and sensible for the business? Do the hyperlinks work, or do they bring us to a defunct 404 error page? Is mobile speed optimal? Does the website function easily, or does it take the visitor on loops of clicks?

Social Media Links and Ecosystem

To maximize the impact of social media platforms, it's essential for businesses to interlink their social media accounts, creating a cohesive and viral ecosystem of digital communication. By connecting social media platforms—Instagram, Facebook, X, and other "digital campfires,[5]" like Discord or even video games such as Fortnite—businesses can enhance cross-platform promotion and engagement. For instance, a post on Instagram can be shared on Facebook, or a tweet can direct followers to a blog post on the company's website. This interconnected strategy helps build a unified online presence, making it easier for followers to engage with the brand across various platforms. Moreover, it encourages the organic spread of content; users who engage on one platform are likely to share it on others, enhancing the potential for viral reach.

However, it's not enough to simply connect these platforms; the brand must maintain a consistent and cohesive brand identity—such as logo, color scheme, and tone of voice—while tailoring content to suit the specific platform and its audience. For example, while LinkedIn might require a more professional and formal tone for sharing industry insights, Instagram can showcase the brand's visual appeal through creative and engaging images or videos. With its character limit, X is ideal for quick updates and pithy commentary, while Facebook offers a space for more detailed posts and community engagement.

A high-end hotel might use Instagram to highlight luxurious amenities and scenic views, while using LinkedIn to share articles on industry trends or corporate partnerships. A festival might employ Snapchat or TikTok for behind-the-scenes content and live updates, catering to the Snapchat audience. By creating an ecosystem of linked social media channels, businesses can reinforce their brand message and engage with a wider audience.

Think Like a Marketer, Act Like an Owner

As marketers, our role is that of strategist and trusted advisor. Our job is to conduct primary and secondary research to inform the strongest recommendations possible. We analyze the data, explore the trends, and tap into audience insights—always with the goal of supporting business success. However, it's important to remember that we may not be the final decision-maker. The owner or operator may choose to take—or not take—our recommendations. What matters most is that our ideas are grounded in thoughtful analysis and backed by credible evidence.

So, how does an owner think and act? An owner sees every decision through the lens of long-term value, profitability, and viability. They weigh risks and returns, ask tough questions about budgets and payoffs, and consider how each action aligns with the bigger vision for the property or brand. When we, as marketers, adopt this owner's mindset, we don't just pitch creative ideas; we tie them directly to revenue goals, operational realities, and the guest or customer experience. Acting like an owner means caring about the bottom line as much as the brand image and preparedness to defend our recommendations with facts, forecasts, and a clear plan for impact.

Today, tools like ChatGPT and other large language models can help us move faster and even uncover new ideas or sources. But these are *starting points*, not definitive sources. ChatGPT is a powerful text generator, not a fact-checker. While it's commonly used as a search shortcut, it's critical to take an extra step: ask for sources, then verify those sources for accuracy and credibility. Only once we've done our due diligence can we consider including that information in our marketing assessments or plans.

Ultimately, when we present a recommendation, we must be ready to stand behind it with research and rationale. Whether or not our suggestion is adopted, we've done our job: to think like a marketer and act like an owner, with our credible research to support our suggestions.

Marketing Mantras

By taking the time to research, analyze, and ask the right questions, businesses can uncover valuable insights that drive effective decision-making. Conducting the right research ensures we are focusing on key opportunities to better understand competitive landscapes.

1. **Understand Target Audience Through Research:** Effective marketing hinges on a clear grasp of our target audience(s), achieved through quality research. Primary research offers direct insights into customer behaviors and preferences, while secondary research provides broader market trends and benchmarks. Together, they help develop deep knowledge.

2. **Differentiate Between Primary and Secondary Research:** Primary research involves gathering new, firsthand data through surveys, interviews, and focus groups. Secondary research analyzes existing data, such as market reports and competitor analyses, to understand industry trends and competitive positioning.

3. **Ask Targeted Questions to Drive Quality Research:** The quality of research is driven by asking focused questions to uncover valuable insights. Key areas to explore include target market definition, marketing mix evaluation, visibility and brand exposure, timing, lead quality, and media partnerships.

4. **Use SWOT Analyses for Strategic Insight:** Conducting a SWOT analysis involves evaluating internal strengths and weaknesses and external opportunities and threats. This framework provides a rounded view of a company's current position and informs strategic decisions.

5. **Analyze Competitive and Comparable Sets:** Understanding competitive sets (direct

competitors) and comparable sets (similar businesses) is crucial for benchmarking and strategic planning. A detailed SWOT analysis of competitors can reveal market gaps and opportunities for differentiation.

6. **Evaluate Website Performance for a Seamless User Experience:** Evaluating a website's front-end and back-end is essential for ensuring a seamless user experience and optimal performance. Key aspects include navigability, working links, high-quality visuals, readability, calls to action, and mobile responsiveness.

7. **Link and Analyze Social Media Platforms:** Linking social media platforms creates a cohesive digital communication ecosystem. Researching and reviewing social conversations is a valuable tool for analyzing audience sentiment and engagement (sentiment analysis).

8. **Stay Updated on Our (Client's) Digital Presence:** Always check a client's website and social channels, even the morning of a meeting, to show that we are up to date on their digital presence. This demonstrates diligence and professionalism, building trust with the client.

Now that we understand the importance of conducting research and gathering actionable insights, the next step is to master how to communicate those findings effectively. Knowing how to speak and write the language of our audience is as crucial as the strategies we develop.

So let's now explore how to craft compelling messages, present ideas with clarity, and build connections through effective communication, using the vocabulary of a marketer and the industry you represent. Great marketing is about what we know and how well we can convey it to others.

Marketing Mindset in Motion

Every great marketing strategy starts with the right information. Think of a recent business, brand, or marketing decision you've encountered—whether your own or one you've observed. What data or research might have informed that decision? Now put yourself in the role of a strategist. What are three key questions you would ask to gather the right insights before making a move? Consider sources such as customer feedback, competitor analysis, and digital performance metrics. How can better research refine and strengthen your marketing approach?

2

Speaking and Writing the Language of Marketing

How many languages do you speak? It's important to speak in the language of your customer to show connection and interest. In my digital marketing course, I stress the importance of understanding the "language of digital."

I often tell my students that I find it amusing when someone claims to be a digital marketing expert because the rules are constantly changing. However, if someone is working, living, and breathing digital marketing daily, of course, I'm going to trust their expertise more than my own. I stay informed by reading and connecting with professionals in the field, which helps me remain current.

Because digital marketing shifts constantly, I forgo using a textbook and instead rely on real-time articles and simulations, allowing students to explore the material more thoroughly, leading to a deeper understanding.

My goal in teaching digital marketing strategies is
for students to
know enough to be dangerous.

Whether individuals find themselves working for others in a company, a marketing role, or even launching their own business, everyone should be well-versed in the vocabulary and nuances of digital marketing. This foundation empowers us to communicate effectively and make informed decisions in the digital space, knowing enough to contribute wisely and ask the smart questions.

It's important to note that digital marketing today cannot be separated from "traditional" marketing because both are interconnected and essential to a comprehensive strategy. While digital marketing focuses on online platforms, social media, and data-driven tactics, traditional marketing, such as print ads, direct mail, and TV, still plays a vital role in reaching different audiences. Today, the lines between digital and traditional marketing are blurred, and both need to be integrated to effectively communicate a brand's message and drive results.

Applying the Language

Classroom Cases

Here are a couple of classroom examples of when our students needed to speak the language of marketing to professionally share their recommendations with our clients.

From Stagnant to Stunning: Revitalizing a Legacy Restaurant's Digital Presence

Student: Namrata Sridhar

School: Boston University School of Hospitality Administration

Graduation: Class of 2019

The Marketing Challenge: The class was tasked with conducting a digital audit and providing recommendations for Boston's legacy seafood restaurant brand, Legal Sea Foods. Nammi and her team were solely dedicated to assessing the efficacy of the company's website. In that process, our class friend Todd Philie of Southcoast Marketing Group ran an overall report, scoring the Legal website at 74 out of 100 for overall effectiveness. The score considered the quality of the content, the search engine optimization (SEO), and the user experience.

Outcome: Nammi and her group recommended installing a crawler, a bot that bridges website links to Google servers to boost the site's SEO. This would increase the likelihood that, when someone searches online for "best seafood restaurants in Boston," the restaurant appears among the top three listings shown beneath the local map. Secondly, the team indicated that menus online were more optimizable from HTML than from a PDF. Students suggested retyping the menu into the text for stronger optimization. Looking at the direct competitors, the team noted that other restaurant menus were online and included delivery options, too. Google searches for competitive restaurants indicated which keywords were visible in search ads, such as "New England clam chowder" and "steamed mussels." This was important because the restaurant was not showing in the top results spots for essential food and beverage searches. It matters, as the students explained, because the chances of web visitors searching beyond page one on Google decline dramatically.

Namrata's Insight: "The ability to certify in Google AdWords and Search not only allowed me to distinguish myself in job interviews but also equipped me with a robust grasp of KPIs, metrics, and overall digital marketing strategies. Since graduation, I have successfully applied these competencies in developing comprehensive paid search and social media campaigns for a company. I continually refer to the principles learned in both the digital and strategic marketing courses as fundamental elements of my professional success. These experiences have shaped my career path and have also underscored the enduring value of knowing how to speak the language of digital."

# # #

Serving Warmth: A Three-Part Content Series Bringing Comfort to the Table

Student: Lawrence Mannix

School: BU School of Hospitality Administration

Graduation: Class of 2021

The Marketing Challenge: When Lawrence was a student (prior to his work as my teaching assistant) in the digital marketing course in the spring term of 2020, the teams were asked to conduct digital assessments and create a three-part video content series for a restaurant. Lawrence's team selected MIDA as their restaurant subject. MIDA is an Italian neighborhood restaurant, known for local generosity and the "desire to host a great meal shared with friends." Under the direction of Chef Douglass Williams and his business partner, BU School of Hospitality alum and faculty lecturer Seth Gerber, MIDA has grown in the Boston area and in the hearts of locals for the warmth it conveys.

Outcome: Lawrence and his team, taking the brand values important to Chef Douglass and the vibe he wanted to convey, created a three-part video series for the restaurant, with the overarching theme of "warmth." The three video components were titled "Warmth through Food," "Warmth through Service," and "Warmth through Community." The intention was for the restaurant to utilize the three-part series for social media posts, YouTube content to enhance SEO, and even for internal training and morale building.

Lawrence's Insight: "When I joined my (previous) company, there was an initial period of onboarding. And I really appreciate this lesson from our classes in college: It was so important to learn the terms, acronyms, and vocabulary of the company and culture. It is helpful for all involved, in sales or operations, to be fluent in the language of your organization. It made me think of our marketing classes because we learned how to communicate our marketing terms in a manner that our clients could understand. We learned to share our language so that everyone would feel comfortable."

Both Namrata and Lawrence stress the importance of speaking the language of marketing to effectively share recommendations and drive successful outcomes. Nammi's detailed digital audit for Legal Sea Foods showcased how clear, data-driven communication can highlight key areas for improvement, ensuring that clients understand the strategic value behind each recommendation. Similarly, Lawrence's creation of the "Warmth" video series for MIDA illustrates how articulating brand values through compelling content not only conveys meaningful messages but also educates clients on the benefits of cohesive storytelling.

In both cases, the ability to articulate marketing concepts in a clear and accessible manner enabled my incredible former students to bridge the gap between complex strategies and client understanding. By educating, they ensured that recommendations were well received and understood so clients could embrace and effectively implement the recommendations for enhanced digital presence and strengthened community connections. Mastering the language of marketing and fostering client education are essential.

Key Concepts and Terms

As you can infer from our introductory chapters, a marketing mindset means speaking the language and understanding the words to get the job done. As marketers, whether in hospitality or any other industry, we have our own vocabulary and acronyms to speak a language of communication and methodology. It's important to understand the vernacular and use it in our everyday "marketing speak." Here is just a "smidge" of a digital and marketing glossary so we can familiarize ourselves with some of the terms, acronyms, and expressions we use in our marketing analyses and recommendations.

Owned. Earned. Paid.

In the realm of marketing and media, the concepts of owned, earned, and paid media play a crucial role in shaping a brand's presence and communication strategy.

1. **Owned media** refers to channels and content a brand controls, such as its website, blogs, social media profiles, and email newsletters.

2. **Earned media** is the exposure a brand gains through organic means, such as word-of-mouth, public relations, and customer reviews.

3. **Paid media** involves any form of advertising that requires financial investment to promote a brand's message, including digital ads, sponsored posts, and traditional advertising.

   (**Social media** often bridges all three: a brand may own its profile, earn shares and mentions, and pay to boost posts or run ads, making it a powerful tool across the full media mix.)

Together, these three types of media form an approach to brand communication and customer engagement. Each plays a distinct yet interconnected role in building and sustaining a brand's reputation and in shaping our marketing mindset.

While referenced in earlier chapters, there's also the vocabulary of STP:

STP (segmentation, targeting, positioning) is a marketing framework used to identify and reach specific audiences effectively.

- **Segmentation:** The process of dividing a broader market into distinct groups of consumers with shared characteristics, such as demographics, interests, behaviors, or needs.

- **Targeting:** The selection of one or more of these segments to on which to focus marketing efforts, tailoring strategies to meet the specific needs and preferences of the chosen audience.

- **Positioning:** The development of a unique value proposition and messaging that distinguishes a brand or product in the minds of the targeted consumers, ensuring it resonates with their preferences and expectations.

Additional key terms that marketers often use in our conversations include:

- **UGC (User-Generated Content):** Content created by customers, such as reviews or social media posts, which can enhance credibility. Let customers do the talking for us with their podcasts, blogs, videos, or other forms of organic (not paid) digital presence that they share on our behalf.

- **SEO (Search Engine Optimization):** The process of optimizing content to rank higher in search engine results.

- **Paid Search:** Using paid methods (not organic) to maximize online visibility and drive traffic to the website. This refers broadly to advertising on Google, Bing, Yahoo search engines.

- **PPC (Pay-Per-Click):** A digital advertising model where advertisers pay a fee each time their ad is clicked by someone searching the web.

- **SERP (Search Engine Results Page):** The goal is to have a mix of organic and paid optimization methods so our product lands on the first page of the results when users conduct a Google search online.

- **CRM (Customer Relationship Management):** Systems and strategies used to manage a company's interactions with current and potential customers.

- **ORM (Online Reputation Management):** The practice of monitoring and managing a brand's online reputation.

- **WOM and DWOM (Word of Mouth and Digital Word of Mouth):** Traditional and digital forms of spreading information about a brand. Powerful avenues for "getting the word out" or dangerous mechanisms for spreading false information.

- **The Funnel Concept:** Let's recall the earlier pages of this book, as we shared the essence of several marketing frameworks in the Introduction. Remember the marketing funnel? This structure helps us understand the customer journey, from initial awareness to interest, desire, and then action or conversion. Familiarizing oneself with these terms allows us to tailor messaging and strategies to address the specific needs and motivations of prospects at each "stage of the funnel." If we are referring to "top of the funnel" marketing, we mean the start of the funnel, which is the mass marketing, broadcast, or "awareness" phase.

- **Awareness vs. Conversion:** Distinguishing between awareness and conversion metrics is vital for measuring marketing effectiveness accurately. Awareness metrics, such as impressions and reach, gauge the extent of your brand's visibility and exposure, while conversion metrics, such as click-through rates and conversion rates (book now; reserve today), measure the efficacy of your efforts in driving desired actions, such as purchases or sign-ups.

- **Content Marketing Terminology:** Content marketing is an essential element of modern marketing strategies, encompassing a wide array of tactics, from blog posts and social media updates to videos and infographics. Understanding terms like evergreen content (timeless), user-generated content (UGC), and content syndication empowers marketers to create engaging, relevant, and shareable content that resonates with their target audience.

- **Email Marketing Jargon:** Email remains one of the most effective channels for engaging customers and nurturing leads. Marketing professionals must grasp terms like open rate, click-through rate (CTR), segmentation, and A/B (comparative) testing to optimize email campaigns for maximum impact and conversion.

- **Social Media Terminology:** Social media platforms offer unparalleled opportunities for brand building, customer engagement, and community building. Marketers should understand terms such as engagement rate, organic reach, viral content, and influencer marketing to leverage these platforms effectively and drive meaningful interactions with their audience.

- **Before we know it, GEO will be in our vocabulary.** Generative AI Optimization. Conceptually, this would mean the process of designing, structuring, and refining content, prompts, and workflows to maximize the effectiveness, accuracy, and relevance of outputs generated by AI systems.

Words Matter

In the world of digital marketing, success hinges on more than just creativity; it requires the ability to speak the right language, both in content creation and audience engagement. The following cases demonstrate how thoughtful messaging, strategic use of keywords, and digital fluency can transform a brand's online presence and deepen its connection with customers.

Brewing the Right Message: Speaking the Customer's Language for Digital Success

Student: Kim Kibler

School: BU School of Hospitality Administration

Graduation: Class of 2018

The Marketing Challenge: In spring 2018, Kim was my graduate course teaching assistant, and our subject restaurant for the digital audit was Hopsters in the Seaport neighborhood of Boston. Hopsters was a bar, restaurant, and brew-your-own-beer spot, with two thousand square feet of brewing space and four thousand square feet for dining and drinking. It was an honor for us to research and learn to make intelligent recommendations to assist this venue with its launch.

Outcome: Research at the time taught us that (academic. mintel.com):

- 61 percent of beer drinkers were men
- 60.9 percent of consumers were aged twenty-one to forty-four
- 32 percent of U.S. adults perceived beer as affordable

- 34 percent of Millennials preferred brands with a social media presence
- 74 percent of Millennials used mobile to research prior to a purchase decision

The class assessed competitors, including Harpoon Ale, Cheeky Monkey Brewing Co., Rock Bottom Restaurant & Brewery, Saugatuck Brewing Co., and a few others. We then reviewed our own and the competitors' websites and created SWOT analyses for each, including the strength of the user experience of each site on varying devices. Is the website engaging, offering call-to-actions, interactivity, with rich content, captivating copy, and a calendar of events? Are there FAQs available for enhancing the user experience (UX) and boosting SEO? Are the phone number and address clearly visible on the site? Can someone sign up for an email newsletter? Is loading speed optimal on desktop, laptop, and mobile devices? Are the proper keywords used for ads, web copy, and age, location, and time-based targeting? Is the restaurant's presence clear on user-generated review sites, including Google, OpenTable, Facebook, Yelp, or other pertinent review sites and delivery app sites?

Minor enhancements to elevate the social sites, including the use of Snapchat, were suggested. Paid search was highly recommended for creating direct targeting that can be monitored, tweaked, and modified to drive conversions among a geo-targeted audience.

Kim's Insight: "Personalize the message. The great thing about digital is you can automatically change the words appropriate for the audience individuals."

# # #

Finding the Right Search Terms to Elevate a Neighborhood Mexican Restaurant

Student: Paulina Preciat

School: BU School of Hospitality Administration

Graduation: Class of 2023

The Marketing Challenge: How can we ensure that Sunset Cantina's website and digital content are more easily found?

Outcome: The students discovered that the restaurant had opportunities to optimize their website's terms and phrases to elevate their standing on a search results page.

Paulina's Insight: "Use distinguishing terms and keywords. Humanize your digital connection and engagement. These days, we search for places as if we are talking to our friends. Businesses must remember that Google serves the user first. Thus, as the marketer, one must think like the user to build a paid search campaign. People come to Google with questions. The marketer who best answers the user's questions, both pre-click and post-click, will be the most successful one.

"As an example, our digital marketing challenge was for the local Boston University restaurant, Sunset Cantina. We assumed that their SEO was strong (search engine optimization) and that they would appear in the most obvious searches, such as "best Mexican in Brookline" or "best Mexican on BU campus," for example. However, they did not appear in those simple searches. Brands must make the effort to optimize their SEO and use the right words to showcase themselves and answer customer questions. Google likes that, and that will help our search engine ranking when people search online."

There's a common thread that emerges in these two examples: the critical role of using the right language, both in crafting marketing messages and optimizing digital presence. Kim's work with Hopsters highlighted the importance of tailoring digital content and using strategic keywords to align with customer behavior and improve search visibility. Similarly, Paulina's project underscored the necessity of identifying and implementing the most effective search terms to meet users' expectations and improve SEO performance. What we learn from each of these examples is that fluency in the language of the brand and its audience is required. Whether through storytelling, digital audits, or SEO strategy, understanding how to communicate effectively and taking care to use the proper words or vocabulary is key. Words matter.

Elevate Vocabulary

Language encompasses both the specific vocabulary of the industry we're marketing and the broader context of marketing itself. I emphasize the careful selection of words that elevate our presentations and writing and convey intelligence. Here are a few of my personal pet peeves and a few tips:

- **Avoid lazy words.** Words like "huge" or "big" lack specificity. Use more precise alternatives, such as "significant," "impactful," or "meaningful." Or better yet, use statistics for more specificity and a stronger imagery of what you want to communicate. There are several (what I call) "lazy verbs," as well. Instead of relying on generic verbs such as "to do," "to make," "to have," and "to be," opt for more descriptive action words. There are so many other wonderful words in the English language to elevate our writing for stronger professionalism.

- **Use positive phrasing.** With respect to sharing marketing recommendations, I encourage others to frame instructions positively to improve clarity and foster a more engaging tone. I prefer language in the positive tense, rather than the negative. Writing in a positive tense can make communication clearer and more impactful by focusing on what can be done rather than what should be avoided. Negative phrasing can often lead to confusion and a subtle sense of discouragement, simply because it emphasizes what is not desired or should not happen.

For example, instead of saying, "Don't forget to submit your assignment on time," a positive phrasing would be, "Remember to submit your assignment on time." The latter is more direct and encourages action rather than avoiding a mistake. Similarly, rather than instructing someone with, "Don't leave the door open," it's clearer and more constructive to say, "Please close the door." This approach not only avoids potential ambiguity but also fosters a more optimistic and proactive mindset. By framing instructions and statements positively, we create a more inviting and motivating atmosphere. Perhaps this language of positive tone stems from my graduate school training in public relations.

- **Avoid (what I call) "dirty words."** In the realm of marketing recommendations, certain dirty words can be particularly unwelcome to business owners who are focused on maintaining the prestige and value of their offerings. I do not allow these words in my classroom or in the student assessments of their client marketing.

  o The words "cheap," "bargain," or "low-cost" can be detrimental, as they often imply a lesser quality or lower value product, which can undermine the brand's positioning and perception. Similarly, terms such as "basic" or "standard" can be undesirable, as they may suggest a lack of uniqueness or differentiation in the market.

o D is for discount. It's also for don't. Don't say discount in my class. Instead, position our offer as "special pricing," "limited-time offer," or better yet, a "value-add" experience.

Owners often prefer language that emphasizes the unique features, quality, and experiences associated with their product or service. They aim to create a perception of value and exclusivity, rather than relying on cost-cutting measures. An owner does not want to hear that their product or service is discounted. Unless we're trying to quickly reduce inventory to make room for new products, a valuable service needs to retain its brand and rate integrity. So, to act like the owner, focus on enhancing the overall customer experience or unique amenities to more effectively resonate with the target audience. I do not allow "discounts," "vouchers," or "coupons" as recommendations in my classes. If there's a "value-add," that's great. No discounts. Not in my classes. Not in my client work.

o Often, age information is needed for gathering data, but let's avoid using age in messaging. I'm an anti-agist; if "age 55+" is the last box on a market research survey, you have just earned an F. Today, there are active sixty-year-olds, seventy-year-olds, eighty-year-olds, and yes, ninety-year-olds who are traveling, staying in hotels, and dining in restaurants. I also don't want to hear the words "old" or "elderly." I challenge you to find other ways of saying "experienced," "seasoned," or "veteran." How can we emphasize wisdom, expertise, and the value of experience rather than age? I know it's my hang-up, but when someone says they are too old to do something, it makes me cringe.

Clothing brands, hotel brands, and luxury goods can be marketed based on a person's wants and desires. It's not about age. As for price point, today consumers can spend on a one-time luxury item so that price is no object, or for others, the high-ticket item is an aspirational spend or experience, and that's what's meaningful. Likewise, a "mock-product" (think Walmart's Wirkins bag mimicking the famed Hermes Birkin bag), while completely priced for affordability and available through an approachable marketplace, can also serve as a status symbol for value-conscious luxury. Take care in how we word our marketing.

○ Avoid using "handicapped." It's outdated and often seen as disrespectful. Instead, use inclusive language, like accessible entrance, accessible restroom, person with a disability, or be specific if appropriate (for example: wheelchair user, person with low vision). When in doubt, focus on describing the access feature, not labeling the person.

o Hotel Packages? No. Use the word experiences. Let's avoid commoditizing our hospitality or service offerings; it risks diminishing the value we bring. While terms like package or bundle may make sense operationally, what the guest should encounter is something special and thoughtfully curated. That's how we should position it: not as a transaction but as a memorable, meaningful experience.

- **Avoid filler words in our writing.** Unnecessary conjunctions appear frequently, and we often fail to notice this. The tighter version of "Can you speak up in class?" is "Can you speak in class?" Better yet, "Can you participate in class?" And please do not conclude a sentence with what I call a "dangling phrase, conjunction, or preposition." For example, please write, "Where are you going?" and not, "Where are you going to?"

Writing Tips

Here, I share a few more suggestions I teach for improved writing. These are simple and easy to implement:

- **Concise. Precise. Entice.** What do I mean? Is your text brief, yet with sufficient descriptors or supporting points for effective writing? Is it specific enough to effectively tell a story and create a visual image of the information? Is it reader-friendly and engaging? Is it clear?

- **Edit the fluff.** Cut the extraneous, unnecessary words, particularly for a business document, such as a marketing plan. This type of writing is not intended to be poetic, academic, or creative. It is professional.

- **Use graphics, charts, and illustrations.** A marketing plan is a professional business document that is easier to read when paragraphs are shorter, bullet points flow logically, and charts, graphs, or images are used to illustrate examples or key points. A visually appealing read makes for an easier and more digestible action plan. This will entice the reader to continue through the plan. Of course, details should be included but presented in a way that's easy on the eyes. Owners do not have the time to read a long narrative. Get to the point.

- **Vary the vocabulary.** Avoid repetition of words in the same sentence and, if possible, the same paragraph. Find synonyms or other ways of rephrasing and rewording to create an interesting sentence. Sentence variety is also important. Avoid using sentences with similar structures in the same paragraph. If we read "noun, verb, action" repetitively, sentence after sentence, it sounds choppy and immature. Owners want a quick and easy read of marketing and business plans, so a well-structured, nicely formatted, and legible narrative is key.

# # #

I also emphasize, reiterate, and encourage the following:

- An incremental approach to writing assignments, advocating for a process that begins well before the deadline. Starting early allows for ample time to develop and refine ideas without the pressure of a looming deadline. I encourage students to write a draft, then step away from it for a while. This break provides a fresh perspective when they return, revise and expand on their initial thoughts. I encourage students and others to apply this philosophy to our writing, recognizing that working on a piece gradually allows for deeper reflection, thoughtful revisions, and greater overall clarity.

- Additionally, I urge students to involve others in the process. Having a friend read their work or reading it aloud themselves can provide valuable insights into the clarity and flow of their writing. This practice helps identify awkward phrasing or unclear sections, ensuring the final piece is coherent and engaging. It also allows students to develop and refine their ideas over time, resulting in a more polished and thoughtful final product.

- Shorter paragraphs are easier to read and help us register, comprehend and digest information more effectively.

- Use bullet points to create clean and clear formatting. This is especially helpful when delivering complex documents, like marketing plans to hotel or restaurant owners, clarifying the content and improving navigation. I also advise varying vocabulary and sentence structure, along with the proper use of punctuation, to maintain the reader's interest and ensure clarity. These strategies collectively enhance the readability and professionalism of any written work. When using bullet points, ensure the list contains between three and five items, making it easier for readers to remember. Confirm that each item in the bulleted list begins similarly with a noun or a verb, for example, and avoid repeating the same starting word to create a fluid, readable list.

- *Ensure every piece of marketing communication includes a clear call to action (CTA).* Whether it's an email, a social media post, or website content, the reader should know exactly what to do next: book now, reserve today, download here. In emails, explicitly guide the recipient by offering clear options (for example, "Would you be available at one of these three times?") and prompting them to confirm. A strong CTA encourages engagement, facilitates conversions, and ultimately helps achieve the intended marketing goal.

Writing Tips in Action

The Taj: I recall a Harvard Business School (HBS) case study I taught called Taj Hotels, Resorts, and Palaces. The case is about the intended launch of Taj's Vivanta brand in India at the time of the horrific terror attack at the Taj Mahal Palace and Tower in Mumbai (2008). Students had a challenging time writing this paper because Indian Hotels Corporation Limited (IHCL) is the parent company of Taj Hotels, Resorts, and Palaces (THRP). Tata Group is a conglomerate with numerous publicly listed subsidiaries, including IHCL. Sentences were more confusing when referring to "Taj," the overarching name for the company, or "The Taj," the individual property in Mumbai, not to be confused with the Taj Mahal.

It can get confusing, but even composing this paragraph demonstrates the importance of clarity and revising sentences until the information and names are communicated effectively. And as difficult as it was not to repeat the name "Taj" in a sentence, I'd urge the students to read the sentence aloud to hear how awkward and unpleasant the sentence was with all the repetition.

Rephrase. Rewrite. Find synonyms.

Feeding Creativity: Using Art to Draw Lunch Patrons to a Seaport Steakhouse

Student: Ally Rung

School: BU School of Hospitality Administration

Graduation: Class of 2017

The Marketing Challenge: Del Frisco's in Boston's Seaport aimed to grow its lunch business by showcasing its striking artwork and impressive collection of magnum bottles as unique draws for diners. How can we promote other aspects of such a special space to encourage lunch-time business?

Outcome: The team reached out to local artists with galleries or offices in the Seaport neighborhood (again, hyper-local connection) and the Institute of Contemporary Art (ICA) to explore cross-branded opportunities. Additional promotions were designed for specific outreach to Uber and Lyft drivers for broadening local awareness and developing relationships with drivers who are in positions to influence their passengers about dining options.

Ally's Insight: "Throughout college, I was not a great writer—horrendous, actually. We were tasked with three to four papers throughout the course, and on the first two or so, I averaged a 75 percent. My writing was choppy, and I wasn't writing effectively for my audience. I quickly learned key writing skills that I still use in my public relations job today. These lessons included simple items, such as sentence structure, to more high-level themes, such as storytelling through words. I learned how to edit my work and rewrite sentences until they were completely clear. I would even read my work aloud to friends, and if they understood the story I was trying to tell, I knew I had written that paper correctly.

"In the field of PR, strong writing skills are necessary for a successful career. I continue to use these simple hacks to keep improving. I also continue to think like a marketer when writing: *How would my client best receive that email?* or *How would that journalist best receive a pitch?*"

Ally's insight emphasizes that well-crafted writing is essential in marketing communications. Reading your work aloud helps ensure your message is clear and resonates accurately with clients, enhancing the effectiveness of your recommendations.

Speaking Tips

Speaking of speaking, let's talk about the art of speaking and presenting for a moment. It is critically important for a marketer to articulate their message smoothly and eloquently, interestingly and passionately, and accurately and clearly. Our students read *Talk Like TED*, Carmine Gallo's dissection of the successful patterns of effective

TED speakers. This helps us prepare for our marketing pitch because there are nine tips that Gallo shares:

To evoke emotions:

1. Deliver your insight with passion.
2. Master the art of storytelling.
3. Have a conversation.

For an original or striking talk:

4. Teach people something new.
5. Deliver jaw-dropping moments.
6. "Lighten up."

And for a memorable presentation:

7. Stick to the eighteen-minute rule.
8. Paint a mental picture with multi-sensory experiences.
9. Stay in your lane.

More on this in the "Presentation Skills" chapter because it is critically important. Just note, I read the first three chapters of *Talk Like TED* every August as a beach read to rejuvenate myself and prepare for the semesters ahead.

Bringing the Destination Home: Online Experiences When There's a "No-Travel" Restriction

Student: Danielle Galea

School: BU School of Hospitality Administration

Graduation: Class of 2021

The Marketing Challenge: During the pandemic, the Greater Boston Convention & Visitors Bureau (GBCVB), now known as Meet Boston, challenged students to develop a comprehensive marketing action plan promoting the city as an ideal destination for "staycationers."

A staycation is a vacation where individuals or families choose to stay at home or within their local area rather than traveling to a distant location. During a staycation, people engage in leisure activities typical of their traditional vacation, such as visiting local attractions, dining out, enjoying outdoor activities, or simply relaxing at home. The idea is to take a break from the usual routine without the hassle or expense of travel.

Outcome: Encouraging families, groups, or solo travelers from Massachusetts to travel in Boston during the time of the pandemic was a tough challenge. Danielle and her team conducted primary research through the Qualtrics survey software to determine consumer sentiment toward travel in the Northeast region of the United States in October of 2020. This geographic area was selected due to state travel restrictions and the rise in domestic and local travel during the pandemic. The survey received 228 responses of varied demographics; respondents were sourced through two channels: Amazon Mechanical Turk (MTurk) and via social media outreach (i.e., Facebook, Instagram, Snapchat followers).

Although 26.98 percent of survey respondents were motivated to travel as a means to escape quarantine, 20.93 percent reported they were "not willing to travel at all." When asked specifically about traveling to Boston for leisure during the pandemic, only 11.01 percent expressed a strong willingness to visit without hesitation. A larger portion felt indifferent (25.23 percent), while 21.56 percent were firmly opposed to leisure travel to the city at that time—signaling notable hesitancy around urban destinations.

Interestingly, Gen Z showed the most enthusiasm for Boston leisure travel, with 26.9 percent indicating a high willingness to visit in October 2020. On the other hand, the most reluctant groups included Baby Boomers (39.19 percent), parents of children over eighteen (34.21 percent), and parents with younger children under eighteen (31.25 percent).

The team recommended numerous virtual experiences, including cooking classes, concerts, family events, and even Christmas celebrations. Paid search is a targeted and cost-effective way to promote the virtual, online experiences. If we build a website, we need to direct people to it. We can use online search or display ads to respond to Google searches with click-throughs to landing pages for a personalized call to action.

Danielle's Insight: "I loved the *Talk Like TED* assignment. I'm a third-grade teacher now, so it's important to be effective and strong in presenting information to my young students. I loved that there was a bit about 'mastering the art of storytelling' to reach people's hearts and minds. The book explains how brain scans show stories stimulate the brain. Another interesting point shared in the book was the concept of introducing novelty into the presentation—either by packaging the same information differently or introducing something entirely new. As a teacher, it's important to keep third graders entertained and engaged, so I incorporate storytelling and novelty into all my lessons now. My kids just eat up the stories and are much more engaged when storytelling is involved."

Danielle reminds us, as does the *Talk Like TED* outline, that exceptional presentation skills, including effective storytelling and engaging delivery, are crucial for career success in any profession, enabling individuals to captivate their audiences and clearly communicate their ideas.

Marketing Mantras

1. **Use Clear, Positive, and Precise Language:** Well-crafted communication helps convey our message effectively and strengthens our brand.

2. **Focus on Value-Driven Messaging:** Let's avoid language that diminishes brand value—what I call "dirty words"—such as cheap or discount. Instead, we should emphasize messaging that highlights quality, trust, and long-term benefits.

3. **Adopt the "Concise. Precise. Entice." Mindset:** When we write, we want to assure our communication remains compelling and professional.

4. **Continuously Refine Speaking and Presentation Skills:** Great communication isn't just about writing; it's also about how we speak and present our ideas.

5. **Commit to Lifelong Learning in Marketing:** Language and marketing trends evolve constantly, and so must we.

Mastering the language of marketing is about ensuring that every word and action conveys clarity, purpose, and value. Whether we're crafting digital strategies, conducting audits, or delivering pitches, effective communication is at the core of what we do.

This foundation of precise and impactful communication sets the stage for our next chapter: exploring why strong internal communication is essential and should happen first.

Marketing Mindset in Motion

Words shape perception, and in marketing, they can make or break a message. Look at a recent marketing email, ad, or social media post from a brand you follow. How effective is the language? Are there weak or filler words that dilute the message? Now, rewrite it with stronger, more precise, and persuasive language. How does your revision change the impact?

Inside to Out: Internal Communications Before External

B oy, is this a concept I continually repeat to clients and to students in the classroom. The importance of communicating to internal audiences before external ones cannot be overstated. This is a principle I often repeat in class because I want our student teams to ensure they consider employees, stockholders, boards of directors—all internal stakeholders—as an important target audience for any marketing message. Communicating marketing strategies, campaign objectives, and key messaging within the company fosters a sense of ownership, collaboration, and commitment across departments, from sales and customer service to operations and finance. Employees should have pertinent information before guests or other external stakeholders do.

Internal Communication:

- Ensures alignment among all departments
- Fosters employee advocacy and trust in the brand
- Prevents mixed messaging and miscommunication with external audiences

My Sheraton New York Examples

What does it mean to communicate internally first, then externally? Here's a very simplistic example I tend to use in my classes for ease of understanding:

- Imagine your hotel has a Valentine's weekend package (sorry—not a package anymore, an experience). Guests call the hotel to book their experience, but the front desk or reservationist isn't aware of any special rate or promotion. Yet, the guest read about this Valentine's promo in their local newspaper or through social media posts. Wouldn't it have been prudent to share the information with the internal team first, before it was shared with the public? Keep employees and other internal stakeholders informed in advance to demonstrate competence, and ensure all information is accurate.

- Many moons ago, when I worked for Sheraton Hotels in New York, we were about to embark on a $100 million renovation of the two properties on 7th Avenue in Manhattan. As the public relations department, working closely with our human resources department (which facilitated internal communications), it was important that we informed all employees in all their spoken languages about the extent of the renovation at hand. We then created scaffolding around our building (with photographs of our employees[6]; yes, they made it to Broadway!) to help get the word out to our neighborhood about our renovation, new name, and timeline. Both our employees and our local community were important internal audiences for us.

- In 1992, at the conclusion of the $100 million renovation, the hotels changed names after several decades of long-established legacy. During the renovation, repositioning, and rebranding period, another important audience—a priority external audience for us to reach—was the local taxi driver community of New York City. We organized a week of taxi driver promotions to gift clipboards (remember this was in the 1990s) and flyers with our new name. We also offered complimentary coffee to all the cabbies who stopped by our hotel during those morning hours. These "local influencers" were an important audience for us to reach and help spread the word of our new name. But can you imagine if the taxi drivers knew about the new name before the hotel employees did?

# # #

Classroom Cases

These two classroom cases highlight the critical role of internal communications as the foundation for effective external messaging, ensuring alignment and trust among stakeholders before engaging broader audiences.

Building the New Brand from Within: Internal Comms Lead the Way for Hotel Repositioning

Student: Marut Raval

School: Boston University School of Hospitality Administration

Graduation: Class of 2020; MMH Class of 2021

The Marketing Challenge: Owner, Fidelity Investments, was to embark upon a significant renovation of the Seaport Hotel, which would result in a complete repositioning and rebranding. Due to COVID, plans changed, and the repositioning did not occur. However, while the students were working on "the repositioning and marketing plan," the goal was to determine how, when, and what to communicate with existing guests, corporate clients, the local industry, meeting planners, travel agents, tour operators, and prospective customers. This was a global marketing and messaging effort, not all that different from my experience with Sheraton Hotels in New York decades earlier.

Outcome: The students developed an actionable communication plan and timeline—a thorough and realistic working document that clearly emphasized the need to reach internal audiences before external. The hotel general manager and executive team were so appreciative of the structured and comprehensive plan that they asked the students to return to the hotel and present to the Fidelity ownership directly.

Marut's Insight: "Internal before external. This was the crux of our Seaport marketing plan. Everything ties together. We had to act like owners for our marketing plan. If we solely thought like marketers, we would have developed an external communication plan and just called it a day. The internal communication plan was key to the execution of a major multi-million-dollar renovation. The staff, from management to the line staff and service workers, all needed to be on the same page."

Earning Trust: How Respect and Appreciation Strengthened Stakeholder Cooperation for Success

Student: Maura Feltault

School: Boston University School of Hospitality Administration

Graduation: Class of 2017

The Marketing Challenge: The Massachusetts Convention Center Authority (MCCA) sought to enhance its relationship with local hotels to better accommodate future conventions. How can we effectively collaborate with hotel sales teams to ensure they help the MCCA confirm rooms and rates years in advance? It's a common challenge, but not an easy ask of hotels.

I shared a little about this project earlier in the book, and I wanted to share yet another perspective.

Outcome: Maura and her teammates interviewed hotel sales departments to understand how requests for future room bookings, made years in advance, are perceived and managed. A very important lesson the students gleaned: the importance of saying "thank you." Hotel sales departments indicated that resentment was building because the continued requests of the MCCA for convention hotel rooms, while important for future business, were made without sensitivity or appreciation for the hotels needing to report to their respective owners. Or, if sales teams had booked the rooms, which was good for business, the MCCA didn't clearly thank them for assisting with the request. A simple "thank you" is the difference between feeling appreciated and valued, rather than taken for granted and feeling used.

Maura's Insight: "My team worked with the MCCA to improve hotel relations and drive occupancy to the hotels for their future convention business. The hotels needed to put trust in the MCCA to hold an inventory of rooms for large association business booked to come to Boston, way out in the future. For our project, we proposed a two-pronged approach, both internal and external, for the MCCA to implement. I remember this as an important lesson in realizing that what you say and believe in your internal communications is not always how it is perceived by others. Clarity is key."

Together, these projects demonstrate that internal communications set the tone for external success.

Benefits of Effective Internal Communication

Why is internal communication so critical, and why is it important to manage prior to external outreach? There are numerous reasons, and here are several to get us thinking:

1. **Employee Engagement and Advocacy:** Engaged and informed employees are our most valuable brand ambassadors. By keeping internal teams

abreast of marketing initiatives, brand values, and customer feedback, companies can empower employees to embody the brand promise and deliver exceptional experiences at every touchpoint.

Example: Imagine an employee who feels uninformed about a new initiative. They are less likely to confidently convey the brand's message to customers. In contrast, well-informed employees become natural brand ambassadors, confidently sharing updates with customers and their networks.

2. **Mitigating Miscommunication Risks:** Misalignment between internal and external messaging can undermine brand credibility and erode customer trust.

   Example: A new product is launched with a unique feature, but if internal teams don't have clear details or proper training, they may provide conflicting information to customers. Clear internal communication prevents such inconsistencies and ensures a unified message across all touchpoints.

3. **Training and Education Initiatives:** Investing in ongoing training and education initiatives ensures that employees stay abreast of industry trends, best practices, and evolving marketing strategies. Whether through workshops, webinars, or online courses, providing opportunities for professional development empowers

employees to excel in their roles and contribute to the company's success.

Example: A restaurant chain introduces a new menu item that requires staff to explain its ingredients to guests. Without adequate training and education on the product, servers may fail to upsell or provide a positive dining experience, delivering value in every interaction.

4. **Feedback Loops and Continuous Improvement:** By soliciting feedback from frontline staff, managers, and executives alike, companies can identify blind spots, address challenges, and refine marketing strategies for optimal effectiveness. Establishing feedback loops allows employees to share insights, voice concerns, and contribute ideas.

   Example: A hotel front desk staff member notices that guests frequently ask about parking rates, but this information is buried on the website. Creating a feedback loop allows the employee to suggest adding parking details to the FAQ section, improving the guest experience, and reducing frustration.

5. **Crisis Preparedness and Response:** By clearly guiding employees on responding to customer or media inquiries, companies can maintain trust, transparency, and control over the narrative.

   Example: During a negative PR event, such as a customer complaint going viral, employees may panic if they're not informed about how to respond. Even if the guidance is simply to refer all inquiries to the designated spokesperson, a well-communicated crisis plan enables employees to know exactly who to contact, what to say, and how to manage the situation effectively.

6. **Cross-Functional Collaboration:** Marketing success requires collaboration across departments, from product development and sales to customer service and finance. A culture of collaboration and cross-functional teamwork can leverage diverse perspectives and talent to drive business growth.

   Example: When marketing launches a campaign promoting a hotel's new loyalty program, but operations isn't informed about how to implement it, the guest experience suffers. Effective internal communication ensures all departments work together to deliver a seamless customer experience.

7. **Consistency in Messaging:** By ensuring that internal and external messaging aligns with brand values, positioning, and voice, companies can reinforce brand authenticity, credibility, and trustworthiness across all communication channels.

   Example: A luxury resort chain rebrands to emphasize sustainability. If the marketing department promotes eco-friendly practices externally while internal teams aren't aware or trained on the new standards, it creates confusion. Consistency in messaging is key.

8. **Celebrating Successes and Milestones:** Whether through team meetings, company-wide announcements, or recognition programs, acknowledging the contributions of individuals and teams fosters a culture of appreciation, pride, camaraderie, and excellence.

   Example: A retail chain hits a major sales milestone, but employees don't hear about it. Without recognition, morale can drop. Conversely, publicly celebrating the achievement through an internal announcement or event boosts morale and motivates employees to strive for future success.

9. **Empowering Employee Advocacy:** Encouraging employees to share company news, promotions, and content on their personal social media channels amplifies the reach and impact of marketing efforts. Providing guidelines, resources, and incentives for employee advocacy, companies can harness the collective influence of their workforce to amplify brand messaging and strengthen engagement.

   Example: A hotel launches a social media campaign and encourages employees to share the content on their personal channels. Employees who feel engaged and informed about the campaign are more likely to advocate for the brand, amplifying its reach and credibility.

10. **Continuous Learning and Adaptation:** Staying ahead of the curve requires a commitment to continuous learning and adaptation. Fostering a culture of curiosity, experimentation, and learning agility can empower employees to embrace change and drive innovation in marketing communication strategies.

Example: A tech company introduces a new customer service chatbot, but the technology evolves rapidly. Without a culture of continuous learning, employees may struggle to keep up with changes. Encouraging ongoing learning ensures staff remain adaptable and ready to embrace innovations.

Measuring Internal Communication

Measuring internal communication effectiveness is as important as the communication itself. Just as external marketing efforts are evaluated based on key performance indicators (KPIs), internal communication effectiveness should be measured and monitored regularly. Surveys, feedback mechanisms, and engagement metrics can provide valuable insights into employee satisfaction, comprehension, and alignment with organizational goals.

When we approach internal communication with the same strategic mindset as external marketing, we ensure that the entire organization is aligned, engaged, and empowered to deliver a consistent and compelling brand experience—a critical component in learning to think like a marketer.

Effective Use of an Internal App

Clear Communication for a System-Wide Health Care Rebrand: One of the articles I instructed the class to read was the January 2016 *Long Island Newsday* piece by Ken Schacter, introducing and telling the story of the renaming and repositioning of the North Shore and Long Island Jewish Medical Centers to today's Northwell Health. The process of redefining the original two hospitals to reflect the healthcare system they had become took nearly ten years. The goal was to broaden their reach beyond New York and engage internal stakeholders to secure buy-in. While unusually long, the process, as described in this newspaper article, was deliberate and thoughtful. CEO Michael Dowling seemed determined to cover all the bases in the process to ensure the powerful board of trustees and significantly sized team of clinicians and staff were kept informed and looped into discussions.

The process of renaming, rebranding, and repositioning was critical; it was important to get it right. Between 2008 and 2015, four external consultants were retained, and five thousand names had been formally or informally considered for the new company.

One of the tools used to assist with internal communications was Northwell's development of an app to connect with the system's nearly 3,000 physicians, 15,000 nurses, and 13,600 doctors with admitting privileges (in 2016). Months before the external launch of the new name and value proposition, Michael Dowling and Northwell's new (at the time) chief marketing officer, Ramon Soto, introduced the brand via the internal app, myNorthwell, which soon after revealed the healthcare brand's new logo.

This case illustrates that large-scale organizational changes require extremely clear internal communication as well as innovative tools, such as Northwell's app, to ensure consistent messaging across a vast internal network.

#   #   #

What's in a name? As previously stated, it's not easy, but it is important to get the name right. In the case of Northwell, above, the healthcare giant was growing and dropped its name, which tied it to Long Island to brand it more strongly as a regional healthcare system. The challenges in finding the right name were numerous. Narrowing five thousand options to six hundred and then to three involved extensive research, linguistic analyses, and legal reviews. This process was managed while the board of trustees was hesitant to change the name in the first place because the North Shore-Long Island Jewish hospitals were so deeply entrenched with such a strong foundation and reputation. A great deal of persuasion and engagement was needed for Dowling and Soto to succeed in moving forward while retaining the legacy of the hospitals. The efforts clearly succeeded.

And the name Northwell works very effectively. It keeps the "north" from the original name and location. And looking "north" means looking "up," doesn't it? North "well" communicates the "wellness" that the system wants to share. The brand is not just about hospitals taking care of people as needed, but also taking care of people at all stages of life. The Northwell name works very well. It's hard, but it's important to get it right.

Marketing Mantras

1. **Begin With Internal Audiences. They Come First.** Effective marketing begins within the organization. Informing employees, stakeholders, and other internal groups first ensures alignment and a cohesive message before reaching external audiences.

2. **Build Employee Engagement and Advocacy.** Engaged employees are powerful ambassadors. When employees understand the brand's goals and messaging, they can authentically represent the organization and provide exceptional experiences.

3. **Prevent Miscommunication.** Aligning internal and external messaging mitigates the risks of confusion or contradictory narratives, helping preserve credibility and customer trust.

4. **Create Feedback Loops for Improvement.** Internal communication isn't one-sided; encouraging employees to share insights and feedback refines marketing strategies and uncovers potential blind spots.

5. **Foster Cross-Functional Collaboration.** Successful marketing requires collaboration across various departments. Engaging cross-functional teams maximizes perspectives and resources, ensuring holistic execution of strategies.

6. **Ensure Consistency. It is Key.** Internal communication ensures that all team members understand and embody the brand's voice and values, creating a unified and trustworthy message externally.

7. **Drive Crisis Preparedness Through Internal Communications.** Proactively informing internal stakeholders during times of crisis equips them to manage external inquiries effectively.

8. **Celebrate and Engage Internally.** Recognizing employee contributions to marketing milestones fosters pride, loyalty, and a culture of excellence that strengthens organizational unity.

9. **Measure and Improve Communication.** Just like external marketing, the effectiveness of internal communication should be measured using surveys and engagement metrics to ensure alignment with organizational goals.

Let's approach internal communication with the same strategic mindset as external marketing. Before we can effectively communicate outward, we must ensure that our internal teams are well-informed, engaged, and aligned. In the next chapter, we'll explore how social listening, personas, and strategic positioning help us craft relevant, personalized messaging that resonates. After all, the most well-communicated message means little if it doesn't reach the right people in the right way.

Marketing Mindset in Motion

Before a brand delivers a message to the world, it must first communicate it clearly within. Think about a company you admire; how do you imagine they align their internal teams before launching a major campaign? Now, consider a workplace or brand where communication has fallen short. What impact did that have on the external message? If you were leading the internal rollout of a new marketing initiative, what steps would you take to ensure clarity, alignment, and enthusiasm before going public?

Marketing Mindset in Motion Scorecard

Now is a terrific time to pause and reflect. Let's think back to the structures shared in our Introduction and the key takeaways from the last three chapters.

This scorecard is designed to help us assess growth as we read *Marketing Mindset in Motion: Inspired by Hospitality.* By engaging with the key concepts from the previous chapters, we recognize that marketing is not just a function but a dynamic, strategic mindset—one that integrates research, communication, and intentional decision-making to drive meaningful business outcomes.

How to Use This Scorecard:

- **Self-assess**: At the end of each section, rate yourself on a scale from 1 to 5 in the designated categories.

- **Reflect**: Consider the questions under each milestone to gauge how well you're applying the concepts.
- **Evolve**: Adjust your marketing mindset as you progress, revisiting earlier chapters when necessary.

Milestone: From Understanding to Application

Introduction Part 2, and Chapters 1, 2 and 3.

Concept	1 (Needs Work)	3 (Getting There)	5 (Fully Integrated)
Applying Marketing Frameworks	I know of frameworks but don't apply them effectively	I use frameworks but struggle to connect them to strategy	I apply frameworks strategically to shape marketing decisions
Research-Driven Decision-Making	I rely on assumptions over data	I gather research but struggle to interpret insights	I use research to drive well-informed marketing strategies
Communicating InternallyBefore Externally	I focus only on external marketing	I recognize internal alignment matters but don't prioritize it	I ensure internal communication aligns with external messaging

Now think about the following questions. How would you respond?

- Are you integrating marketing frameworks into your decision-making?
- Do you rely on data to shape marketing strategies instead of assumptions?
- How do you ensure internal messaging supports external marketing efforts?

4

Know Your Audience: Personas, Positioning, and the Power of a Marketing Mix

James Beard award-winning chef and restaurateur Jody Adams once said in our Future of the Restaurant Business class, "Fall in love with your customer, not your product." That's a great way to ask how our product meets customers' needs. How do we know we are truly providing the customer solution? Don't you just love her quote? It's so good.

Target marketing allows companies to tailor their messages, product offerings, and overall strategy to resonate deeply with specific customer segments. By narrowing the focus and understanding audience nuances, companies can enhance relevance, engagement, and long-term loyalty. Here we will explore how target marketing, when combined with a diversified marketing mix, can improve brand relevance and resilience. We'll uncover how marketers can craft detailed personas, leverage data for precision targeting, and build a mix that ensures long-term success. This means we need to know our audiences. Who is our customer, and why are they using our product or service?

Target Marketing

Recollection and Reflections

Targeted marketing is critical because it allows businesses to modify messages and offerings to resonate deeply with specific audiences -- maximizing relevance and engagement. Keep in mind that achieving sustainable growth requires a balanced marketing mix to broaden reach and diversify impact. These three reflections highlight the power of targeted marketing, personalization, and strategic efficiency to craft impactful campaigns, even when resources are limited.

# # #

Laughs, Leads, and Limited Resources: Crafting an Actionable Venue Marketing Strategy for a One-Person Team

Student: Jamie Weber

School: Boston University School of Hospitality Administration

Graduation: Class of 2020

The Marketing challenge: Jamie's team managed the proactive marketing for Laugh Boston and Improv Asylum, sister comedy clubs in Boston's historic North End and Seaport neighborhoods, which were not well known at the time. The venues offered space for special events as well as group rates for comedy shows. Awareness and reaching new audiences were important for the marketing effort. Improv Asylum had more consistent sales for shows and brought in extra business with corporate trainings and customized shows at private events. Laugh Boston was a newer club, which produced fewer but higher profit events.

At the time, the events manager handled all outreach for both venues, so recommendations must be efficient and manageable by one person.

Outcome: The students shared best practices to help the events manager distinguish the two venues while marketing their cooperative opportunities and shared ownership.

Jamie's Insight: "Targeted marketing is key. You simply can't be everything for everyone, no matter how universal your product or service may be. Instead, it is crucial to segment your target market to ensure you are precise about who you are looking to reach and how you're going to reach them. This is important for advertising, public relations, sales promotion, digital marketing, and personal selling. We can focus our energy and resources on that persona through surveys and research, so you can thoroughly understand who they are and how they want their information and communication.

"This project taught us how to use humor because it was aligned with the brand. And the target marketing helped distinguish sister brands while also fostering collaboration and synergy. The project also taught us how to focus on efficiency when resources are limited."

# # #

"Personalization in marketing is no longer a luxury; it's an expectation. Digital tools give us the incredible ability to adapt instantly, flipping a switch to adjust strategies and meet individual needs in real-time. This agility ensures that every interaction feels relevant and impactful." – Kim Kibler, BU Hospitality, BU School of Hospitality Administration, Class of 2018.

These insights demonstrate how clear focus, creativity, and adaptability can enhance target marketing success while fostering meaningful connections with audiences.

Social Listening

Social listening and sentiment analysis are other methods to build target market personas. Monitoring mentions and discussions on social media platforms can surface common pain points, emerging trends, or overall attitude toward a brand. Analyzing this qualitative data provides insights into how customers truly feel and what they might need next.

Sandra King is the founder and principal of STKing Associates, a marketing strategy firm. She also serves as a lecturer at Boston University's Questrom School of Business, where she teaches courses in service marketing and consumer behavior. In the May issue of the Boston University School of Hospitality Administration's *Boston Hospitality Review*, Sandra and I chatted about social listening. Sandra emphasizes the importance of listening to customers and adapting to their behaviors to succeed as marketers. She adds that social listening is on the rise, so businesses can "better understand the chatter about their companies, products, and services." Listening is key.

Sandra identified Dove as a brand that clearly "has the pulse on its customers." The company "engages, listens, and responds to consumer sentiments, as is evidenced in their brand messaging strategy about young women in their early and mid-teens and their shifting self-confidence and self-image. They [Dove] have also run campaigns on aging and skin care targeted to their audience—women advancing through life. They use accurate size models and strive to make their products relevant and relatable to the average consumer across cultures."

Personas

To effectively market to our audience, we must first understand them. So, we create personas to better understand their needs, wants, and desires. In the context of creating a marketing plan, a persona is a fictitious, detailed representation of a specific segment of the target audience. It is built using a combination of demographic, psychographic, and behavioral data to encapsulate the needs, preferences, and motivations of a group of potential customers. Personas help marketers humanize and better understand their audience, allowing for more precise and effective marketing strategies.

Why Personas Matter: For classroom purposes, I always recommend that students identify a market mix of three distinct personas because it encourages a broader, yet focused, approach to targeting. By defining three specific audience profiles, students are compelled to think critically about diverse customer needs and how to address them uniquely. This approach also ensures the marketing plan isn't overly generalized, allowing for customized strategies that resonate deeply with each distinct group. The goal is to create campaigns that feel personal and relevant while still maintaining efficiency in reaching multiple segments.

The Significance of the Customer Persona: *"It was so helpful to create the information for our personas—our three target audiences. From a communications standpoint, it helped us understand when they want communication and what they want to know. Our personas provided richer insights than demographic data alone, helping us identify our target market's challenges and position ourselves as the solution. I use this concept all the time, especially for something as important as an email blast to our members or community neighbors. What subject line or message is important to them, so they open my email? Hyper-segmenting our lists into interest groups helps us enhance our ability for continued effective communication."* Elise Borkan Macklin, BU School of Hospitality Administration, Class of 2019

# # #

A balanced marketing mix can be achieved by first identifying your primary market (e.g., business travelers), then developing strategies for secondary markets (e.g., families), and finally exploring tertiary markets (e.g., event planners). Each segment should have a distinct strategy while maintaining overall brand consistency.

When building personas, it's important to consider various types of segmentation to capture the full spectrum of a target audience's characteristics. Below is a quick guide to common segmentation types with examples.

Type of Segment	Definition	Example
Demographic	Based on age, gender, income, etc.	Young professionals aged 25–35
Psychographic	Based on lifestyle, values, and interests	Health-conscious, eco-friendly
Behavioral	Based on purchase patterns, brand loyalty	Frequent travelers, repeat buyers

MMGY's EVP Julie Freeman reminds us that "by using data and analytics to better understand target audiences, marketers can create a more targeted, customized approach, personalizing campaigns that are relatable to the consumer."

Businesses can use data and analytics in a variety of ways to gain deeper insights into their target audiences and build personas. Some examples include, but are not limited to, the following:

1. **Gathering Demographic Data:** By collecting information such as age, gender, location, and income, businesses can segment their audiences into meaningful groups. This segmentation helps them craft messages that resonate with each audience's specific interests and needs.

2. **Leveraging Customer Behavior Metrics:** Tracking metrics like website clicks, email open rates, or

purchase patterns can highlight which products, services, or content pieces appeal most to different segments. These patterns reveal which marketing efforts drive engagement and conversions.

3. **Implementing Analytics:** Predictive models use historical data, such as purchase history or online behavior, to forecast future actions. This helps businesses proactively modify offers or recommend products based on each customer's likelihood to respond or buy. For example, a hotel chain could use predictive analytics to forecast when repeat customers are likely to book their next stay, enabling targeted promotions during that period.

4. **Conducting A/B Testing:** Testing different versions of ads, emails, or landing pages (for instance, changing headlines or visuals) can reveal which elements resonate best with certain groups. This data-driven optimization ensures messaging aligns precisely with audience preferences. Like the example above, an A/B test could help determine which email subject line ("Limited-Time Offer" or "Book Now for Exclusive Rates, for example) drives higher open rates.

5. **Assessing Customer Lifetime Value (CLV):** Analyzing the total value a customer brings over time reveals which segments are most profitable or loyal. With this data, marketers can prioritize their efforts and budgets on audiences that deliver the greatest return.

All this information will help build a better understanding of the personas. And data analysis is never a one-and-done process. Continued tracking, using dashboards or analytics tools, helps businesses adapt their marketing strategies as audience preferences shift.

Sample Personas

Sample personas, such as those developed by my industry friend JoAnne Borselli and her colleagues at Connelly Partners in Boston, offer valuable insights into understanding and engaging diverse target audiences. These personas were created as part of a strategic effort to redefine the appeal of a well-known historical destination in the U.S., moving beyond its traditional reputation to position it as a must-visit location for travelers of all types. By "dimensionalizing" the target audience, Connelly Partners aimed to expand the destination's perception, fostering repeat visits and broader appeal. These personas exemplify how thoughtful audience segmentation can drive innovative marketing strategies.

The agency analyzed secondary sources and crafted five personas for their destination client: "contemporary explorers," "history buffs," "adventure seekers," "nature enthusiasts," and "slow-paced travelers."

The *contemporary explorers*, for example, are described as passionate travelers "who thrive on curiosity and cultural immersion. They love discovering both cultural spots and hidden gems, "planning meticulously while valuing flexibility." Each trip for this persona, is also a journey of personal growth. They immerse themselves in local culture, cuisine, and form deep connections with people and places.

This description tells us that this target market has a strong affinity for cultural enrichment and culinary adventures while looking at each trip as a chance to learn more about the world and themselves.

The contemporary explorer also has a point of view about what they seek in a travel destination. They crave a "local perspective (not just a tourist experience). They want to attend and experience local events and festivals or celebrations happening during that time frame, and they want to travel to a destination that doesn't just have the culinary or the relaxation or the historical appeal. They want a destination that has it all."

The *history buffs* on the other hand are time-travelers who quest for exploring the past during their own journeys. Their travels are "intellectual adventures." They seek historical significance resulting in a trip that is an educational experience for the entire family. They possess intellectual curiosity, consider themselves in-depth explorers and seek authenticity.

These personas help us imagine two of the five target markets and are helpful descriptions (especially when accompanied by visuals) to guide us for effective marketing.

Hospitality and tourism marketing giant MMGY Global provides a complimentary tool online called TRIPs, available at solutions.mmgyglobal.com/trips/. This is a "go-to solution for travel audience segmentation, offering access to precisely defined audience segments for marketers" in a multi-faceted and multi-dimensional world of travel and tourism (all downloadable for free).

Market Mix

Imagine you hold a basket. The basket only has one egg in it. If the basket drops, the egg falls and breaks. There are no more eggs in the basket. Now imagine a basket of five eggs. The basket falls, two are cracked, and fortunately, three are still great to cook with. We need to have more than one egg in the basket.

A robust marketing mix with at least three distinct personas or target audiences is essential for building a sustainable business strategy. Diversifying the audience base ensures that if one segment is adversely affected by external circumstances, our business can rely on others to maintain stability. It's a safeguard against over-reliance on a single group and allows for resilience in the face of market shifts or unforeseen challenges.

I learned this lesson firsthand when my colleague, Eydie Shapiro, and I conducted a sales assessment of a conference center in Connecticut. We discovered that nearly 90 percent of the hotel and conference center's business was dependent on a single pharmaceutical company; in other words, this hotel only had one customer egg in its business basket. When we spoke with the meeting planner from that company, we uncovered serious tensions with the hotel's director of sales, leading the client to nearly pull their business entirely. This situation highlighted the inherent risk of relying too heavily on one market segment or one customer. It was the only time in my career where due diligence and assessment led to someone being let go, but the stakes were that high.

To prevent a business catastrophe, we immediately acted to mend the relationship with the pharmaceutical company while simultaneously working with the sales team to attract new clients and reduce the company's share of the overall business. By diversifying the client base, we not only preserved the hotel's financial health but also protected it from future risks tied to over-reliance on a single source. This case screams the importance of a diversified marketing mix; having multiple personas ensures business stability and growth in an unpredictable market.

Message Positioning to the Audience

As stated, one-size-fits-all messaging does not work. To truly resonate with our audiences, we must shape our messaging and brand positioning for each of our target personas. Each persona represents a distinct segment of our audience with unique needs, motivations, and pain points. By customizing our approach, we create content and experiences that feel personal and relevant, fostering deeper connections and driving higher engagement. The four Cs approach introduced earlier reinforces this by shifting our perspective from simply marketing a product to positioning it as a solution for our audience. Instead of focusing on what we offer, we communicate why and how our product or service meets their needs, aligning our messaging with what truly matters to them.

- Customizing messaging doesn't mean abandoning consistency; it's about maintaining a unified brand identity while adapting our tone, emphasis, and solutions to address each persona's specific priorities. For example, a budget-conscious persona might respond best to messaging that highlights cost savings and value, while a luxury-focused persona would connect with language that emphasizes exclusivity, quality, and premium experiences. The core brand promise remains the same, but the way it is communicated shifts to meet each audience where they are.

- Relevance is key for effective marketing. Audiences are more likely to engage with content that feels geared to their needs and aspirations. By leveraging insights into each persona's behavior and preferences, we can craft campaigns that attract attention and build trust and loyalty. For instance, a persona of "young professional" might engage with dynamic social media content and career-oriented solutions, while a seasoned traveler might prioritize reliable service and expertise in the messaging they receive.

- Targeted messaging also strengthens brand recall and differentiation. When each persona feels seen and understood, they are more likely to associate the brand with solutions that matter to them.

Ultimately, crafting personalized messaging for each persona ensures we remain relevant, competitive, and connected, aligning with the unique values and needs of our audience to lasting relationships across multiple customer groups.

Individual Personalization

Target marketing lays the groundwork for individual personalization, creating stronger emotional connections because it speaks directly to what matters most to each customer:

- A targeted approach enables businesses to craft their messages and their product offerings, promotions, and customer journeys. For instance, a fitness brand targeting young professionals can offer time-saving workouts and mobile app functionality while simultaneously refining content for older customers to focus on health benefits and low-impact exercises. By aligning messaging and offerings with individual needs, brands enhance their relevance and impact.

- Individual personalization allows for dynamic adaptability. With digital tools, businesses can use real-time data to adjust their marketing strategies in real time, ensuring customers receive timely, contextually relevant content. A hospitality company, for example, can use location data to send travel tips to a frequent flyer or offer exclusive promotions to a loyal guest based on their booking history. This ability to "turn on a dime" and provide personalized solutions boosts customer satisfaction and brand affinity.

- Target marketing also increases the efficiency of personalization efforts. By narrowing the focus to well-defined personas, businesses can ensure that marketing dollars are spent on strategies most likely to yield results. Instead of casting a wide net and hoping for engagement, brands can direct their efforts toward crafting experiences that drive conversions.

Ultimately, personalization powered by target marketing is not just about meeting customer expectations; it's about exceeding them. By demonstrating an understanding of who their customers are and what they value, brands can cultivate meaningful relationships that translate into long-term loyalty, advocacy, and success.

Strategic Positioning

In today's extraordinarily competitive business world, generic marketing strategies no longer suffice. To stand out and thrive, companies must embrace strategic positioning through segmentation and hyper-segmentation, rather than attempting to be all things to all people. Here are a few benefits of hyper-targeting your marketing:

1. **Enhanced Personalization and Relevance:** Hyper-targeting allows businesses to deliver personalized messages and experiences that resonate deeply with specific audience segments. By understanding distinct needs and preferences, companies can create campaigns that drive engagement, loyalty, and conversion.

2. **Maximized ROI and Reduced Waste:** Focusing on high-potential audience segments ensures efficient allocation of marketing resources, minimizing the waste that comes with mass marketing. This precision results in a higher return on investment and cost-effective campaigns.

3. **Improved Customer Experience:** Customizing products, services, and communications to specific segments creates a more compelling customer journey. Personalization fosters stronger

emotional connections and boosts satisfaction, encouraging repeat business.

4. **Competitive Differentiation:** Hyper-targeting helps brands carve a unique niche by addressing overlooked or underserved segments. This distinction reinforces the market positioning.

5. **Data-Driven Insights and Agility:** Hyper-segmentation relies on analytics and predictive modeling to uncover audience behaviors and preferences. This data enables businesses to stay agile, adapting quickly to changing trends and refining strategies for optimal effectiveness.

6. **Cultural Relevance and Micro-Moments:** By acknowledging cultural and demographic nuances, businesses can deliver contextually relevant messages that capture attention during those critical "micro-moments," when consumers are most ready to engage.

7. **Long-Term Growth and Ethical Considerations:** Hyper-segmentation fosters stronger customer relationships and brand loyalty, driving sustainable growth. Businesses must, however, prioritize transparency and ethical practices in data usage to maintain consumer trust (and align with regulatory standards.

Customized. Relevant. Creative.

Targeting, according to friend and colleague Marc Mazodier, professor of marketing at the ESSEC Business School in France, must be extremely on point and relevant to connect with an audience:

> "Customization, relevance, simplicity, and creativity are key. Remember that consumers do not pay attention to commercial messages. Average consumer exposures are less than one second to online and outdoor ads, less than two seconds for print ads, and the average viewer only pays attention to 7.7 percent of TV commercials. In other words, viewers gaze at thirty-second commercials for only 2.3 seconds on average. Therefore, marketers must either achieve their communication goals in very short exposure durations or persuade consumers to pay more attention to ads. To achieve the first goal, marketers must focus on simplicity, clarity, and consistency. It is doable to positively impact brand awareness, salience, and familiarity in less than one second, but target consumers must be able to recognize the brand and the offer. To achieve the second goal, consumers will watch longer ads if they are customized, relevant, and creative."

Reimagining Marseilles: Shifting Perceptions and Standing Out in a Sea of European Destinations

Student: Pierre Lego

School: ESSEC Business School, IMHI Hospitality Program; Cergy, France

Graduation: Master's Class of 2024

Marketing Challenge: Marketing the city of Marseilles, France, as an appealing tourist destination is, in fact, a challenge. There are image perceptions to overcome, including a reputation/stereotype of a crime-ridden city. With cities such as Paris, Nice, or Cannes, there are also a multitude of competitive locations within France, let alone throughout Europe, appealing to domestic and international tourists. The city's social and cultural complexity can adversely impact some tourists, yet Marseilles is a rich city with a historic port, ancient architecture, modern neighborhoods, and contemporary developments. The students took a methodical approach: to help rid the negative reputation, to appeal to a new customer base, and then to increase the tourism revenues.

Marseilles is the oldest city in France, originally founded around 600 BC by Greek settlers from Phocaea. The city, therefore, has a multi-layered cultural tapestry that blends ancient history with modern vibrancy. And this was helpful in the recommended marketing messages.

Outcome: The student recommendations were positive and supported by data. For example, the perception of crime was strong, but the facts spoke otherwise. By finding the positive attributes of this complex city and communicating specific benefits of the destination to targeted audiences, the overarching campaign built by the students boosted Marseilles as an appealing travel getaway for French domestic visitors. The city has culture, a great culinary scene, and wonderful beaches. The slogans proposed were: "Marseilles. It always seduces." And "To see France, you must visit Marseilles." The personas created by the team included: young active Parisians, repeat visitors, and wellness enthusiasts.

Pierre's Insight: "A location can be undesirable to some people, while it can be very desirable to others. This is the essence of target marketing and positioning.

"This resonated strongly as my team strived to help change the unfounded perception of Marseilles as a crime-ridden city. Through a thorough analysis, we decided to focus on the Marseilles lifestyle—a slow approach, living by the seaside, with its own vibe and aura. We wanted Marseilles to disassociate from the reputation of crime and drugs. We wanted to tie it favorably to the sea, with fresh Mediterranean foods and other symbols connected to a beach way of life.

"Our team's recommended 'repositioning perspective' proved invaluable during my apprenticeship in customer service relationship marketing for French Railway

Catering. The choices we make in food service and project execution often face criticism as unhealthy or environmentally harmful. To counteract the negative perception, we introduced new products such as plant-based milks and even redesigned our packaging to minimize environmental impact. These initiatives have successfully helped us begin to reposition our train's bars as 'conscious' and to some extent, more 'sustainable.'"

As Pierre's case illustrates, the power of customized, relevant, and creative approaches in successful target marketing can address perceptions, identify unique attributes, and personalize messaging to appeal to distinct audience segments. The project highlights how thoughtful targeting can redefine a destination's appeal and position it competitively.

Marketing Mantras

By embracing targeted marketing, creating detailed personas, and diversifying your marketing mix, businesses can improve both relevance and resilience. This approach helps reach the right audiences and ensures long-term stability by minimizing over-reliance on a single segment.

1. **Embrace a Balanced Market Mix:** Relying on a single audience segment is risky. By diversifying into at least three distinct personas—or more— we can broaden our reach, reduce vulnerability, and foster long-term stability.

2. **Build Detailed Customer Personas:** Constructing detailed personas using demographic, psychographic, and behavioral data is essential for truly understanding customer needs, motivations, and pain points. This leads to more precise and effective campaigns.

3. **Keep Analytics Up to Date:** Analytics must be continually updated. Ongoing tracking, predictive modeling, and A/B testing allow us to refine our personas and ensure that strategies remain aligned with ever-changing consumer behaviors.

4. **Monitor Social Media for Insights:** Social media discussions can reveal shifting sentiments, emerging trends, and customer pain points. By monitoring these conversations, we can respond dynamically and shape messaging that resonates with current needs.

5. **Mitigate Risk by Diversifying:** The Connecticut conference center anecdote illustrates the peril of overreliance on a single client or segment. A robust marketing mix—serving multiple audiences—helps protect revenue streams and ensure long-term stability.

6. **Modify Brand Positioning for Each Persona:** View the brand or product through the lens of each target audience to ensure the message resonates strongly with each group of people. This doesn't mean we are tweaking the positioning; it means we are understanding our audience's

needs and tweaking the message for higher relevancy and impact.

7. **Adopt Hyper-Segmentation for Efficiency and Impact:** Hyper-targeting smaller, high-potential groups maximizes ROI by focusing resources where they matter most. This approach also helps differentiate our brand in crowded markets.

8. **Focus on Customer-Centric Solutions:** When brands genuinely listen to their customers—like Dove did in its campaigns—they better align product features and promotional messages with real customer needs and cultural nuances, which strengthens loyalty and trust.

9. **Personalize While Maintaining Brand Consistency:** Personalization involves tailoring tone, emphasis, and solutions to different personas while maintaining a unifying brand promise. Consistency across all segments helps reinforce brand identity while catering to individual preferences.

10. **Prioritize Clarity and Creativity in a World of Short Attention Spans:** Consumer attention spans are fleeting. Our marketing must be clear, concise, and creative to emerge from the crowd, especially online and in fast-paced media environments.

> Trying to be everything to everyone
> means you are nothing to anyone.

As we conclude our exploration of knowing your audience, it becomes evident that understanding their needs, preferences, and behaviors is foundational to effective marketing. The insights gained about our audience will enable us to strategically position our brand in ways that capture attention and drive engagement.

In the upcoming chapter, we will delve into the power of physical and digital visibility, examining how experiential marketing and thoughtful brand positioning can transform the way audiences perceive and interact with our brand. By ensuring that we are visible where it matters most, we can forge deeper connections with our audience, ultimately leading to increased loyalty and success.

Marketing Mindset in Motion

Effective marketing starts with knowing exactly who you're speaking to. Choose a brand you admire and define a key customer persona for them. Is that persona based on interests, lifestyle, or pain points? Some products are based on age. Is this one? Now, think about your brand, product, or service. Who is your ideal customer? How would you position your message to speak directly to their needs, wants, and emotions? The more specific you are, the more powerful your marketing will be.

5

The Power of Physical and Digital Visibility (and, of course, AI)

Build and they will come. Nope. "They" need to know about it. See it, touch it, taste it. Find it in the neighborhood or online. If you build it, then communicate and connect it, then they may come. Visibility, both physical and digital, is critical for a brand's success. Whether it's a restaurant tucked into a bustling city street or an online store vying for attention in a crowded marketplace, being seen and recognized by the right audience is essential. Physical and digital visibility work together to create lasting connections, drive customer engagement, and build brand loyalty, resulting in effective marketing.

Experiential Marketing and the 7Es

Dr. Wided Batat, a professor and expert in experiential and digital marketing, brings deep insights into customer engagement across the retail, luxury, food, wellness, and tourism sectors. Through her innovative approach to global and digital customer experiences, Professor Batat shares a strategic framework that bridges offline and online touchpoints. Known as the experiential marketing mix (7Es), the model reshapes how brands can create meaningful and lasting connections with audiences.

Dr. Batat asks, "Why do some brands make us feel good, while others frustrate us? What drives our connection to certain brands? What makes us buy the same products, return to the same stores, or revisit familiar destinations?"

In her 2019 book *Experiential Marketing: Consumer Behavior, Customer Experience, and The 7Es*, Dr. Batat introduces us to those 7Es—experience, exchange, extension, emphasis, empathy, emotional touchpoints, and emic/etic process—a consumer-centered paradigm designed to help companies create meaningful, profitable experiences that blend physical and digital realms (phygital). Batat advocates for shifting from a product-centered approach to an experience-focused one[7], using the 7Es to craft more relevant, emotional connections with customers in offline and online environments.

The 7Es encourage marketers to prioritize customer-centric and experiential elements, moving beyond traditional product-centric models to foster more enduring connections with audiences. What is the meaning behind the 7 Es?

1. **Experience:** To build customer loyalty, brands must design memorable, multisensory experiences that go beyond the product's function and create meaningful emotional connections.

   Example: A hotel offering guests a signature scent throughout the lobby enhances physical visibility by creating a lasting sensory memory associated with the brand.

2. **Exchange:** This is a two-way, value-driven relationship where brands and consumers share more than transactions, building trust and collaboration for a meaningful bond.

   Example: An online clothing brand offering a live chat service enhances digital visibility by fostering real-time interaction and personalized assistance.

3. **Extension:** Brands can extend their presence across physical and digital spaces (phygital) to create a seamless and cohesive customer journey.

   Example: A retail store launching an augmented reality app enhances both physical and digital visibility by allowing customers to preview products in their homes before purchase.

4. **Emphasis:** Emphasizing specific brand values and messages strengthens brand identity, particularly if aligned with consumers' beliefs and aspirations.

   Example: A café consistently promoting its use of sustainable, locally sourced ingredients boosts its physical visibility with in-store signage and digital visibility through targeted social media campaigns.

5. **Empathy:** Understanding customer needs deeply; empathy allows brands to respond sensitively to consumer desires—vital for fostering a sense of authenticity and connection.

   Example: A fitness center offering personalized workout plans based on member feedback enhances digital visibility through tailored email marketing and app notifications.

6. **Emotional Touchpoints:** Emotional triggers will shape memorable experiences, suggesting brands strategically place these touchpoints to evoke positive emotions throughout the customer journey.

   Example: A restaurant creating a celebratory ambiance for special occasions boosts physical visibility by encouraging word-of-mouth referrals and repeat visits.

7. **Emic/Etic[8] Process:** This approach balances a consumer's internal perspective (emic) with an

external view (etic), allowing brands to understand cultural context and individual experiences, crafting tailored, relevant marketing strategies.

Example: A global hospitality brand offering region-specific services while maintaining a consistent global identity enhances visibility by resonating with both local and international audiences.

Use of the emic/etic process helps brands balance personalized, empathetic marketing with broader trends and insights, enabling them to connect deeply with individual customers while also appealing to wider market segments. With this theoretical, experiential marketing framework in mind, let's explore how physical and digital visibility impact brand engagement and loyalty from a practical perspective and how this impacts our marketing mindset.

# # #

Are you visible? Translating the scientific approach to a mainstream and user-friendly assessment, ask yourself: *Are we visible? Can someone find us readily online? Can a potential customer find enough information about us to answer their questions? Does a customer pass us by because the physical presence of the store entrance is ineffective or uninviting? How can we attract people to our shop or connect virtually and online? How effective is our physical presence? Our digital presence?* A business need not spend exorbitantly or equally in both areas, just wisely and effectively.

Physical Examples

The following brief scenarios exemplify some of the local Boston marketing projects my classes tackled throughout the years, each highlighting how enhancing physical presence—whether through storefronts, events, or in-person experiences—was essential to amplifying digital visibility and strengthening overall brand impact.

- **Scent as Signage:** My friend Noah Danoff, co-owner of Boston's beloved Union Square Donuts, once came to our class for help marketing his brick-and-mortar location in Brookline, Massachusetts. The challenge? Local regulations made traditional signage difficult, which meant many potential customers simply walked right past without ever realizing what was inside.

  Our student team offered a sweet suggestion. Why not use scent as a form of visibility? If the warm, irresistible smell of freshly baked donuts could waft onto the street, it might stop people in their tracks. After all, who can ignore the comforting aroma of a morning donut calling their name? In this case, the scent *became* the sign—an example of physical and sensory marketing working hand in hand to attract attention and drive foot traffic.

- **Music as Mood:** When our students built a marketing plan for the launch of the Newsfeed Café at the Boston Public Library (2016), it was recommended to produce a jazz soundtrack so a tone was set for the café to supplement the rest of its nostalgic branding. Years later, when our class worked with the fitness center Row Republic near the North End neighborhood of Boston, students also recommended advertising on Spotify for awareness of the club, and even developing a Spotify playlist. Both examples highlight how music, whether through ambiance or advertising, can strategically reinforce a brand's identity and connect with its target audience.

- **Attire as Identity:** How are employees dressed in your restaurant? Is there consistent branding reflected in their attire? We collaborated with a vegetarian-friendly restaurant in Brookline, where employees wore anything they wanted to work each day. This lack of uniformity often made it difficult to distinguish between customers and staff. It failed to elevate the service experience, and if the people representing a business don't visually embody or "live" the brand, what message does that send to customers?

  Similarly, one of our student teams once supported a Boston walking tour company called Yummy Walks. The guides were volunteers, and the students not only proposed branded apparel but also designed and modeled it during their final presentation, fully embodying their client's values. Branded apparel acts as walking signage while fostering a sense of community among the volunteer guides. Something as simple as a branded polo shirt or vest can boost the guide's pride and enthusiasm, enhancing the experience for tour participants too.

- **Visibility as Value:** The physical presence of the Earl of Sandwich restaurant on the Boston Common (today a Flour bakery cafe) was noticeable for those inside the park, but its central location created a visibility challenge. Anyone walking along the park's perimeter—where stores, transportation, lighting, and activity were concentrated—would have no idea the restaurant was just a two-minute walk away. Students suggested activities and physical marketing outreach along the park's busy perimeter, targeting the steady flow of breakfast, lunch, and dinner patrons who frequent the area.

- **Activation as Attraction:** At one time, the vibrant Cuban restaurant Casa Caña was located at the lively lifestyle hotel Studio Allston. While the hotel wasn't within walking distance of central Boston or the university campuses, it was worth the Uber ride once you arrived. But how do you attract people to a location that's a little off the beaten path—and keep them coming back? An event calendar was developed and marketed to attract locals and encourage repeat visits. Physical activations, such as events, activities, and festivals, played a key role in enhancing the brand's physical visibility.

- **Packaging as Experience:** My former teaching assistant, and now seasoned digital marketer in Chicago, Kim Kibler, often reminds me of the simple joy of opening an Apple computer box. It evokes the same sense of joyful anticipation as unwrapping a birthday present. While the box serves no real purpose once the computer is in use, many of us keep it. Why? Because it's more than packaging; it's a physical symbol of status and design, a souvenir of the experience Apple so carefully curated. It's our physical remnant of the brand we treasure.

Across these diverse examples—Union Square Donuts, Yummy Walks, Pure Cold Press, Newsfeed Café, Earl of Sandwich, Casa Caña, and even the Apple computer box—one clear theme emerges: Physical presence and sensory experiences are crucial to making a brand memorable. Each brand strategically engaged multiple senses to create distinctive and engaging experiences, whether through visual cues like signage and uniforms, the aroma of fresh donuts wafting through the air, the sound of jazz setting a nostalgic mood, or the tactile pleasure of unboxing a beautifully designed product. Even taste plays a role, from the flavorful offerings that bring customers back to events and cafes.

Union Square Donuts and Earl of Sandwich faced visibility challenges but overcame them by activating senses beyond the visual, using smell and physical outreach to capture attention. Meanwhile, Apple transformed the simple act of unboxing into a multisensory ritual that combines sight, touch, and emotion.

Together, all these examples demonstrate that successful physical branding is more than just appearance. It's about crafting a holistic, multisensory experience to leave a lasting, emotional impact on customers.

Digital promotion (social media ads, email newsletters) will amplify the efforts of physical events and activations. Keep this in mind. They work together.

Hidden in Plain Sight: Overcoming Minimal Street-Level Presence with Signage and Activations

One semester, a student team collaborated with a local bar and restaurant in Boston's Kenmore Square neighborhood, just steps from Fenway Park. The establishment was budget-friendly for students, offering a simple menu, excellent beverages, and a convenient spot for pre- and post-game socializing. Despite its prime location, the bar lacked street-level visibility to attract foot traffic. Its name was clearly displayed above the entrance, but the basement-level door and signage could easily be mistaken for an apartment building rather than a restaurant. The students proposed several strategies to enhance physical presence: outdoor seating on the small front patio during warmer months to create a welcoming, visible space, bunting on the marquee to signal that the restaurant was open and inviting, and hosting special events. These events could include private invitations

for residents and workers or even a block party barbecue catered by the restaurant, held across the street on
the Commonwealth Avenue Mall, to build community
connections. Such activations serve as powerful tools for
increasing physical visibility.

Digital Presence

I often remind students to think about the product or
service and its physical and digital visibility. Does it need
both? Does one or the other need to be enhanced?

Here's a pertinent example. In spring 2020, our projects
suddenly needed to switch directions. For all the hospitality businesses we were marketing, well, we just needed
to stop everything, shift gears, and redesign our marketing for an uncertain and continually changing world.

The following semester, the pandemic remained, and
we were living in a time of severe travel and dining
restrictions. I had called the CEO of the Convention &
Visitors Bureau (now called Meet Boston) in hopes that
the city of Boston was willing to participate in the class; I
wanted our students to help the city in any way possible.
Fortunately, Martha Sheridan said yes and welcomed our
students and project into her extraordinarily busy agenda.

So, here's the challenge: The period of September through
December 2020 meant extremely limited travel capabilities between states. ("Travel bubbles" were formed where

certain destinations welcomed visitors from other specific destinations). Hotels were sitting relatively empty, and restaurants survived on to-go offerings using plasticware and QR-coded menus. So, if visitors cannot come to Boston, how can we bring Boston to the visitor? The Museum of Fine Arts was supposed to host a visiting Monet exhibit during this time. Could it be presented online?[9]

That's when the power of digital presence proved valuable. How can we create authentic Boston experiences online to help visitors feel a connection to the city? Online experiences became significant and necessary to help fill this gap and keep the communication going during what was an uncertain length of time. Airbnb was the first to launch this new phenomenon of online experiences by enabling guests from anywhere around the world to have an experience anywhere around the world. And that's what ultimately resulted: a series of online educational and fun experiences to keep prospective visitors engaged with the destination until the time was right to invite them to travel in person.

We can all appreciate the use of online when we are unable to experience something live. For example, through Airbnb, I gifted an online experience to my husband for Father's Day: a private tasting hour with a master coffee judge in Mexico City for live training and education that also included my coffee-loving children. Our School of Hospitality arranged for a band in Holland to perform via Zoom from the canals of Amsterdam and converse with our graduates during the highly unusual pandemic graduation celebration. Use these simple examples as inspiration for creating branded virtual experiences to supplement the physical presence when necessary. Keep in mind that behind every seamless virtual experience is a complex web of logistics—requiring careful planning, precise coordination, and creative execution.

That same thoughtful execution applies to every element of your online presence, from the structure of your website to the content you use to engage and convert your audience.

- **Website Steps One and Two:** Naturally, one's website is a significant element of a company's online presence. Owners often tell marketers, "Update the website. We need people to book directly, and the latest and greatest information should be there." While keeping our website current is essential, simply updating the website won't automatically drive business improvements. Customers won't know about our updates or fresh content unless we actively guide them to the site. This requires Google paid ads, organic search optimization, email marketing, or direct mail campaigns. And of course, updating the website is only Part A of the equation; ensuring people find and engage with our site is the equally critical Part B.

Landing pages are designed to ensure that consumers and viewers "land" on the most relevant information directly from an online ad. Keep in mind, sending someone to your website's homepage is rarely effective unless the sole purpose is to build general brand awareness. By using targeted ads to direct viewers to a dedicated landing page with specific, relevant information, you significantly increase the chances of engagement or conversion.

On the other hand, if you're using paid ads or email links to drive traffic to your main website, make sure the website is fully optimized and ready to deliver a seamless, user-friendly experience.

- **Rich Media:** This refers to interactive, dynamic content that goes beyond basic text and static images to engage the audience on multiple levels. It typically includes multimedia elements like high-quality photography, videos, animations, audio, and other interactive features designed to capture attention and convey messages in a more immersive way. For example, well-produced videos can tell a brand's story, showcase products in action, or evoke emotions, while professional photography can enhance the aesthetic appeal of a product or service.

Recent data from HubSpot highlights the significant impact of video marketing on consumer engagement and brand perception. In 2024, 89 percent of consumers expressed a desire to see more videos from brands, indicating a strong consumer preference for video content. Additionally, people are 52 percent more likely to share video content than any other type of content, underscoring video's effectiveness in enhancing brand reach and engagement.

Furthermore, 83 percent of marketers utilize short-form video, with 33 percent planning to invest in it for the first time this year. Short-form video also boasts the highest return on investment (ROI) among video formats, making it a valuable tool for lead generation and engagement.

Leveraging rich media and video testimonials to elevate brand visibility is key. Several years ago, through our class, we had the joy of working with Red Apple Lunch. Founded by Lisa Farrell, Red Apple Lunch helps moms provide healthy, delicious meals to their school-age children—delivered directly to schools. The organization partners with local suppliers to source high-quality regional ingredients year-round, prepping and packaging them in ways that are fun, appealing, and nutritious. Designed to support children's well-being throughout the day, the program reflects Farrell's belief in the powerful connection between a healthy mind, a balanced diet, and the role of food in both personal and community wellness.

It's wonderful for our students to work with mission-driven businesses, with an underlying DNA of hospitality, as it builds a positive social impact for the community. The students recommended rich media and took their suggestions a step further to create the video testimonials of school-age children—the best spokespeople for other school-age children—to feature on the website and in social posts, enhancing the brand's online visibility and engagement.

- **Digital Tech:** Even before QR codes were propelled into mainstream usage, their implementation provided a seamless digital experience that customers quickly embraced. Students in our marketing course recommended that management at Saloniki, a fast-casual Greek concept in Boston, implement QR codes to streamline the ordering process. At restaurants like Saloniki Greek in Boston, QR codes made it easy for guests to access digital menus, place orders, and enjoy a contactless payment experience—all from their mobile devices. This technology not only simplified the ordering process but also reduced wait times, allowing Saloniki Greek to serve customers more efficiently and meet modern expectations for convenience. By enabling diners to quickly scan, order, and pay, QR codes have retained their effectiveness as a preferred tool for busy, tech-savvy patrons who value speed and ease.

The use of digital technologies, such as QR codes, has become a powerful tool for elevating the brand experience. They offer seamless access to information, menus, promotions, and exclusive content, enhancing convenience and engagement for customers. Other tools, such as near-field communication (NFC) for contactless interactions (think Apple Pay or Google Pay), augmented reality (AR) for immersive product visualization, geotargeted notifications for personalized offers, chatbots for real-time customer support, and interactive apps for loyalty programs or gamified experiences, further enhance customer engagement. These technologies streamline interactions and provide opportunities for brands to personalize, foster loyalty, and transform everyday interactions into memorable touchpoints.

AI's Role in Marketing: Trends, Workflow, and Trust

This topic is a biggie. There are so many ways to address AI. There is no single, definitive answer to the multitude of questions, except that AI is here, and so let's learn to work with it, ethically, to make us more productive and successful. Here are a few thoughts that immediately come to mind regarding the power of artificial intelligence in marketing. While this is the very tip of the AI iceberg, please remember this is not a book about AI. My friend Michael Goldrich is the right person to author those books. But going forward, we need to think about AI as we further hone our marketing mindset and put it into motion.

AI-driven marketing has emerged as a powerful force in shaping branding, customer relationships, and data-driven decision-making. Brands are leveraging AI technologies to analyze vast amounts of consumer data, predict trends, and tailor their marketing strategies. For instance, Coca-Cola uses AI algorithms to analyze social media sentiment, allowing it to launch targeted campaigns that resonate with its audience and enhance brand engagement.

Personalization, as we've repeatedly emphasized, is another critical area where AI is making significant strides. Retailers like Sephora have embraced AI-driven tools, such as their virtual artist, which allows customers to try on makeup virtually. This innovative approach enhances the shopping experience by enabling consumers to visualize products on themselves before making a purchase, fostering loyalty and encouraging repeat business.

AI technologies have also transformed data-driven decision-making. Netflix, for example, utilizes advanced algorithms to analyze viewer preferences and behaviors, leading to personalized content recommendations. This strategy enhances our satisfaction and significantly improves customer retention rates, because subscribers feel that the platform understands their tastes and preferences.

Automation trends are increasingly shaping how brands communicate with audiences. Companies like HubSpot employ marketing automation tools to segment audiences and deliver tailored content at scale. HubSpot's features allow businesses to send personalized emails based on user interactions, increasing engagement and conversion rates by ensuring that the right message reaches the right person at the right time.

The impact of AI on campaign effectiveness is exemplified by Unilever's use of predictive analytics to enhance its advertising strategies. By determining the best times to reach audiences and the types of content that resonate, Unilever has achieved more effective resource allocation in its marketing efforts, driving better results and increasing return on investment.

Beyond shaping how brands connect with customers, AI is transforming how marketers research, plan, ideate, and present their recommendations. Today, AI tools can rapidly sift through massive datasets, surface hidden patterns, and generate insights that once required weeks of manual analysis. Marketers are using AI-powered platforms to test messaging, simulate scenarios, and even draft campaign ideas, enabling teams to move from concept to execution faster than ever. When it comes to presenting recommendations, AI-generated visuals, predictive models, and dynamic data dashboards help marketers communicate complex ideas clearly and persuasively, elevating the quality and credibility of their strategic proposals.

At the same time, the rise of AI in marketing raises important questions about trust. While AI can boost productivity and reveal sharper insights, marketers must remain vigilant about the accuracy, transparency, and ethical use of AI-generated outputs. Overreliance on AI without human oversight can lead to generic or misleading recommendations that fail to reflect a brand's true voice or values.

> *This makes it critical for marketing teams—and students learning to become marketers—to treat AI as an assistant, not an authority.*

By combining AI's speed and analytical power with human judgment and creativity, we can build marketing strategies that are both efficient and trustworthy.

AI's Role in Distribution and Conversion

My college hospitality marketing professor, the esteemed Peter Yesawich, reminded me of the following insights: AI is also beginning to transform the very core of hospitality marketing: product distribution and conversion. As shared in this book's Introduction, "Marketing Frameworks," we have long worked within the structure of the funnel, imagining prospects moving step by step toward booking. However, as AI tools evolve, we may see this model completely reimagined.

Agentic AI is the term for systems that recommend and act on behalf of consumers. These are systems that are designed to act autonomously, plan, and make decisions to achieve specific goals with minimal human intervention. Agentic AI could fundamentally alter the way guests discover, evaluate, and purchase travel products. Imagine an AI assistant that knows your preferences for wellness amenities, your loyalty status with certain brands, your tolerance for flight connections, and even your favorite beverages at check-in. That assistant may soon bypass traditional web searches, OTAs, or social channels and book directly on your behalf.

For hospitality marketers, this raises profound implications:

- Websites will need to evolve from static showcases into AI-friendly platforms that can communicate seamlessly with digital agents.
- Paid media strategies will shift as AI intermediaries determine which ads, if any, reach a consumer.
- Social media engagement may matter less for mass exposure and more for feeding AI systems authentic, trusted signals about brand relevance and guest sentiment.

- Personalization will move beyond segmentation toward true one-to-one experiences, where AI curates entire itineraries based on nuanced guest profiles.

The implications are clear: Hospitality marketers must prepare for a brave new world where traditional levers of visibility and information-sharing give way to AI-driven pathways of discovery and conversion. Marketers, keep your mindsets open to the possibilities.

Putting AI into Practice in my Marketing Classroom

In my classroom, I remind students that AI, whether it's large language models (LLMs) like ChatGPT, Claude, or others, is not going away. It will only become more powerful and more integrated into how we work. I liken this to the rapid rise of online travel agencies (OTAs), particularly in the post 9/11 years. OTAs shifted from a small experiment to a major force in hotel marketing and distribution strategy. Disruptive, but necessary.

(While AI has the potential to change how OTAs operate—and perhaps even make them obsolete—it will be interesting to see how these platforms adapt to stay ahead of the curve.)

Or consider Airbnb. When it first emerged as an alternative lodging model, many hotels dismissed it as irrelevant and did not even consider it a market rival. Today, major hotel brands have developed (or acquired) their own home-sharing concepts to compete—and while Airbnb might be restricted in some cities, and even banned in others, it's certainly still an active player in the lodging landscape.

Like OTAs and Airbnb, AI is here to stay (though AI may very well alter OTAs and Airbnb). So, we'd better learn how to use it wisely and experiment with it well.

In class, we will sometimes use text generators like ChatGPT to help draft personas (detailed representations of our target audiences) or develop overarching campaign themes by identifying what it is we want to say to our target personas; we use the LLM to connect dots and help us identify overarching and connecting campaigns. We start with clear ideas about what we want to say to our target personas, and AI helps us uncover fresh angles or specific messaging themes.

The key to getting this right is crafting detailed, thoughtful prompts; the more specifics we feed, the more tailored and useful the output becomes. For example, we might ask ChatGPT to generate the persona of a hotel marketing director (for a boutique hotel, a convention hotel, a limited service hotel, or a five-star luxury hotel) and then name that persona (say, your middle name, for example) and then ask that persona—the marketing director— questions based on the nuances and specifications of the hotel or the target audiences. The key is to share information and specifics, so an intelligently crafted persona results from the text generator. The prompt is critical. And of course, we cannot simply take the output at face value. We must use our knowledge to refine and sharpen it for greater effectiveness.

When it comes to writing, LLMs have become an "easy-out" for a lot of individuals. I share clear guidelines with my students for responsible AI use for writing copy.

1. Always check the sources that AI suggests and verify they're credible. Sometimes you click the link, and it's an invalid connection.

2. Cite your sources and remember that AI itself is *not* a source. It's a tool.

3. Revise the AI-generated text in your authentic voice. This way, AI becomes a tool that supports better, faster work, without sacrificing originality or trustworthiness.

As my friend and colleague Laura Davidson, CEO/ Founder of her namesake public relations firm, shared with me, "A tech consultant recently said to me that AI wants to please you with answers, so if it can't find them, it will make them up. These 'hallucinations' can be quite common, so always verify and fact-check." Ask AI to verify and fact-check that its sources are real, and we should always check the sources ourselves.

Before we leave the subject of AI, it's worth looking at how it is being applied today and at how it may soon transform the very fundamentals of hospitality marketing:

The AI Unknowns and What Lies Ahead

One of the biggest challenges in discussing AI is that none of us truly knows the full extent of what changes lie ahead. What we do know is that change is coming, and it will come quickly. For marketers, the best way to prepare is to think innovatively, experiment responsibly, and adapt to the new landscape while also shaping it.

Caution

Despite its advantages, AI has clear downfalls when used in isolation. Algorithms can process vast amounts of information, but they cannot fully capture the nuance of human judgment or the emotional drivers behind customer decisions. Overreliance on AI risks producing assumptions that feel efficient but lack context, leading to strategies that are misaligned with brand values or customer expectations. True effectiveness comes from balancing AI-driven insights with the broader, holistic perspective that only humans can provide.

# # #

The Digital Audit

Our hospitality digital marketing strategies course introduces students to fundamentals. Included in this course is the digital assessment of a hospitality client's online presence. Students are grouped into teams and have a certain digital element to analyze. The process serves as a practical template for any business to conduct its own self-assessments. Please keep in mind that this is a simplified assessment, enough to teach students the essentials. When marketers are in other roles and other platforms are reviewed continually, we re-prioritize the checklist. For now, here's our guide:

1. One designated team of students examines the client's competitive and comparable sets, which include other businesses they compete with or those with similar digital outreach or customer bases.

2. For boosting search engine optimization (organic SEO), a second team will carefully review the website, identifying links, keywords, page count, rich imagery, and calls to action, among other SEO hacks. We also collaborate with our dear friend Todd Philie, whose Southcoast Marketing Group uses a Google tool to measure the effectiveness of a website across various dimensions. This program can determine whether the site includes a site map (which Google values), if

photographs and videos are optimized and compressed for faster loading speed, and how the mobile site performs, among other functions.

Students can key in on the website menu and recommend an About Us or FAQ page, which helps with SEO. Is the text clear and visible for ADA compliance (Americans with Disabilities Act)? Do the sites have SSLs (secure sockets layers) for extra security? (Note the https – not http - at the start of a URL in the search bar.) Are widgets working from the website to sign up for the newsletter or connect to social sites? Does the business have a claimed and optimized Google My Business page?

Today, is our site extremely well-optimized for effective Generative AI outputs during a search?

3. A third team will investigate whether paid search is utilized for a more targeted online presence. Even the smallest budgets can enable a stronger online presence to expand reach and attract new customers.

   The paid search team would also look at e-newsletter distribution (email marketing) and advertising on the online travel agency sites. If the student tests the email and signs up, did they receive an immediate confirmation? Did they receive a newsletter soon after? Did the emails go a step further, and were they personalized?

4. A different team of students will look at the online review sites in our business, such as Google, Expedia, Booking, TripAdvisor, Yelp, Reddit, Beli or other relevant social media, to encourage guests to leave reviews, to ensure reviews are responded to, and to enhance presence in those platforms with hours of operation and crisp, current photography. We also need to listen to consumers and their feedback on sites such as Beli or Reddit (social listening) to stay current with today's consumers.

5. Social media will be assessed to understand the frequency of posts, rate of engagement, and proper voice for each site. Are social posts sponsored to boost reach and expand to new audiences? Does the photography reflect our target audiences and demographics? Families? Students? Seasoned professionals? Foodies?

   Are we creating relevant hashtags for search purposes down the road? Are your contact information and details visible on social sites for easier connection? Does your audience scroll Snapchat or X? Would Instagram make more sense?

   Are influencers involved? How so? Is it helping? How do we know? What are we measuring, and where do we see improvement?

Our students have been so fortunate to have hospitality brands and businesses such as Boston's own George

Howell Coffee, Legal Seafoods, Game On by the Lyons Group at Fenway Park, Hopsters Brewery, Izzy's Steak House in San Francisco, CA, EVOO in Cambridge, MA, and Sunset Cantina on the BU campus as projects open for us to examine their digital footprint and suggest opportunities for improvement. In Paris, thank you to the ownership of Maison Elle, a boutique lifestyle hotel, who was also willing to learn from the hospitality digital marketers at ESSEC.

Students actively engage with these restaurants to understand the brand experience firsthand and then share more intelligent recommendations. We visited George Howell Coffee shop, for example, for the coffee tasting sessions they offered to visitors and locals. Game On, an energetic and fun bar and restaurant at Boston's famed Fenway Park, invited the class to a menu tasting dinner and the chance to play the arcade-like games for a lively and entertaining evening together. Sunset Cantina welcomed us for a late lunch/early dinner to sample the new menu, enjoy the piped-in music, and have a great time. All our experiences meant we knew what vibe we needed to project through our digital recommendations.

This approach is high-level but highly effective and impactful. Leveraging what I call the *Power of Three*, students were encouraged to provide just three key recommendations for each area of review, ensuring that owners could realistically manage the next steps. While there were plenty of suggestions for each segment, narrowing it to three kept the plan focused and actionable.

Our goal was to come across as respectful and constructive—not overly critical or overly confident. Too many recommendations can be overwhelming.

# # #

Mackenzie Miers was a Boston University Terrier basketball player who worked with me as a teaching assistant in her senior year. She loved the opportunity to coach students in digital marketing and was a star in the classroom as well as on the court. Mackenzie reflects:

"One of the most critical components of our marketing education was analyzing the digital footprint of a hospitality business. As part of our coursework, we examined a specific business along with its competitors, focusing on key aspects, such as website navigation, search engine optimization (SEO), front-end and back-end links, mobile responsiveness, and site speed. Our analysis extended to online review platforms like OTAs, TripAdvisor, and Google, as well as assessing the business's social media presence, Google My Business page, email marketing efforts, and even influencer marketing initiatives.

"Conducting an analysis for a real business and sharing simple recommendations for enhancements was such a critical part of our course. This exercise provided practical tools that any of us can utilize in our careers moving forward."

Classroom Cases

Through the years, this course was presented with a variety of marketing challenges that pushed us to devise creative yet straightforward solutions, each aimed at enhancing a business's online presence:

Steaking a Claim: Mastering Digital Tools for a Legacy San Francisco Steakhouse

Student: Joe Johnson

School: Boston University School of Hospitality Administration

Graduation: MMH Class of 2021

The Marketing Challenge: Due to the pandemic, we couldn't visit local restaurants, so we opted to assist BU School of Hospitality alum Samantha Duvall Bechtel, managing partner of San Francisco's Izzy's Steakhouse, with a digital assessment conducted remotely. The restaurant, inspired by infamous bootlegger Izzy Gomez and founded by famed restaurateur Sam DuVall (Samantha's father), has been a Bay Area tradition since 1987. Woven into the cultural fabric of the city, it was a place of alluring, illustrious lore and tradition. The challenge was to assess the restaurant's digital footprint and share recommendations to boost online visibility.

Outcome: Samantha and restaurant publicist Cory Schisler, also a BU Hospitality alum, attended our presentation via Zoom. The key takeaway from the student observations was the need for consistent messaging on various online or social platforms.

Joe's Insight: "Our goal was to analyze a prestigious and historic restaurant in California using all the chapters in our *HSMAI Digital Marketing Guidebook* to devise a set of recommendations that the restaurant could utilize to strengthen its digital footprint. Week by week, we worked in groups through the textbook's chapters, analyzing each lesson and the restaurant's marketing activity. By the conclusion of the course, we collectively presented and explained how the restaurant could make actionable improvements to its digital model via social media platforms, its positioning on Google Search, its website, loading times, search engine optimization (SEO), and overall user experience and accessibility.

"I learned how to effectively use social media, Google, and our website to create a digital marketing outreach ecosystem. I can't express how powerful these tools are. The information in the *HSMAI Guidebook* should be required reading for every business. Period."

Attracting a New Generation of Weddings

Student: Leonie Grundler

School: BU School of Hospitality Administration

Graduation: Class of 2018

The Marketing Challenge: In the fall of 2017, as a senior in the Advanced Strategic Marketing course, Leonie's team faced the challenge of reaching more millennial couples and increasing the number of weddings held at the Mandarin Oriental Hotel Boston (MOHB). The objective was to position this iconic luxury hotel as a top choice for brides-to-be in the Northeast. To achieve this, the team recommended a digital strategy focused on revitalizing MOHB's website, enhancing their social media and search engine optimization (SEO), and engaging millennial audiences effectively.

Outcome: The strategy presented to MOHB was well-received, emphasizing user-generated content (UGC) and influencer partnerships to drive authenticity and engagement. The proposal included allowing bridal parties to take over MOHB's Instagram account on the wedding day, creating compelling user-generated content. This experience had a lasting impact on Leonie's career; she now applies UGC as a core component of her marketing approach at Lioness Games, where it drives significant engagement and broadens digital visibility.

Leonie's marketing strategies today still revolve around UGC, with 95 percent of her ads on Meta (in the last six months) UGC-based, which has been instrumental in driving traffic to her business.

Leonie's Insight: "UGC is the most organic form of content and continues to be a powerful tool across industries. In our Mandarin Oriental Hotel project, we saw firsthand the value of authenticity, as 65 percent of Millennials felt UGC was more genuine than other content, and 86 percent believed it to be a strong indicator of brand quality. This hands-on experience shaped my approach to digital marketing and has been essential in my role as CEO and founder of Lioness Games."

# # #

Finding the Gaps and Identifying Solutions

"Identifying and addressing gaps in our digital marketing strategy has been a cornerstone of my approach as VP of sales and marketing. Our class project examining local business paid search strategies allowed me to draw parallels to our own challenges. When I first began my role, it became evident that our digital presence was outdated and insufficient. Updating our website and enhancing SEM (search engine marketing) efforts were my immediate priorities, driven by the need to improve customer engagement and conversion rates. Integrating an online booking platform was crucial; it not only closed the loop on revenue attribution but also provided actionable insights into campaign effectiveness. This proactive approach, rooted in data-driven decision-making and strategic investment, continues to shape our marketing strategy today, ensuring that every initiative addresses gaps and contributes to our hotels' sustained growth and profitability." Vivian Feinstein-Gough, BU Hospitality MMH Class of 2020, VP Sales and Marketing, SMVNF Ltd. (Grand Caribe Belize, Sunset Caribe, Bananas on the Beach)

From Runway to Reservation: Delicately Elevating the Digital Footprint of a Parisian Fashion-Inspired Boutique Hotel

Student: Alban Sucrot

School: ESSEC Business School, IMHI Hospitality Program

Graduation: Class of 2024

The Marketing Challenge: To reposition the Parisian boutique and lifestyle hotel, Maison Elle, Alban and his classmates examined the potential drawbacks of relying heavily on promotions while assessing a comprehensive view of the hotel's digital footprint.

Outcome: The owner's representative of Maison Elle attended our class session, where students shared compliments, opportunities, and enhancements, team by team and digital topic by digital topic. A critical recommendation for the hotel was the need to eliminate discounting. While discounts can initially attract customers, they may ultimately harm the brand's perceived value by conditioning customers to expect deals rather than unique experiences or exceptional service. The students explored alternative strategies, including forming strategic partnerships and offering value-adds to experiences. The owner's representative was so impressed that the presentation recording was shared with the hotel's owner, who subsequently offered a stipend to anyone in the class to implement the overall recommendations.

Alban's Insight: "The hotel's digital presence needed boosting, particularly to drive traffic to the site, and our recommendations were meant to be two-fold: to strengthen the efficiency of the website and to enhance traffic to it as well."

From legacy restaurants to boutique hotels and international resorts, students applied core marketing principles to real-world challenges and offered fresh, actionable solutions rooted in digital strategy. Whether optimizing a website, eliminating ineffective discounting, or leveraging user-generated content, each project emphasized the power of data, creativity, and strategic thinking.

Simple Steps to Boost SEO and Digital Visibility For Your Personal or Company Brand

Here are some simple steps we can take to improve our online presence and SEO to attract more attention to our brand. This list is certainly not exhaustive. However, it can also prompt us with other ideas.

To Get Started:

1. **Develop a Checklist for Improving a Brand's Digital Visibility:** Create a personalized checklist to ensure ongoing optimization of your digital presence. Include tasks like content updates, SEO audits, social media engagement, and link-building activities to keep your brand top of mind and searchable.

2. **Build an Omnichannel Content Distribution Strategy:** Extend our content reach by distributing it across multiple platforms (blogs, podcasts, YouTube, LinkedIn, newsletters, etc.) while maintaining consistent branding and messaging. Incorporate tracking to measure performance across each channel and refine your approach based on data insights.

   Monitor Analytics and Adjust Strategies: Utilize Google Analytics, Search Console, and social media insight tools to track performance and refine your approach based on what works best. Always *start with the end goals*: know what success looks like and how it will be measured.

Consider These Steps to Promote a Company:

3. **Use Geotargeted Ads to Reach Local Audiences:** Leverage location-based advertising to target specific geographic areas. This helps improve visibility for local searches and increases the relevance of your ads to nearby customers.

4. **Update the Company's Google My Business Profile:** Keeping the Google My Business profile accurate and up to date enhances local search visibility. Include photos, respond to reviews, and update your hours and services regularly.

5. **Link Social Sites to Create a Viral Ecosystem:** Ensure that your social media platforms are interconnected. This not only creates a cohesive online presence but also increases the chances of content going viral by allowing easy sharing across multiple platforms.

6. **Optimize the Website for Mobile Devices:** A mobile-friendly website is critical for both SEO and user experience. Ensure fast load times, responsive design, and easy navigation to keep visitors engaged and improve your search rankings.

7. **Incorporate Relevant Landing Pages with Clear CTAs:** Create dedicated landing pages for specific campaigns, products, or services. Ensure

that each page has a clear and compelling call to action (CTA) to encourage conversions.

8. **Leverage Online Review Sites and Encourage Positive Reviews:** Reviews on platforms like Yelp, Google, and industry-specific sites influence potential customers and search engine algorithms. Encourage satisfied customers to leave positive feedback and respond to reviews to build trust.

9. **Create Rich Media Content to Increase Engagement:** Use a mix of content formats, such as videos, podcasts, infographics, and interactive media. Rich media content increases engagement and sharing, which can positively impact SEO.

10. **Build a Backlink Strategy to Improve Authority:** Focus on earning quality backlinks from reputable websites. Guest blogging, partnerships, and content collaborations can help increase your brand's authority and improve search engine rankings.

11. **Incorporate Voice Search Optimization:** Tailor your content to match conversational queries that users might speak into voice assistants like Siri or Alexa.

12. **Use Consistent Hashtags to Strengthen Discoverability:** Be intentional about using consistent, relevant hashtags across your posts and platforms. Good hashtags help your content get discovered by the right audience and support your brand's visibility. Random or excessive hashtags, on the other

hand, dilute your message and make posts look cluttered or aimless, so choose wisely and use them strategically.

13. **Always Include a Clear Call to Action (CTA):** Every piece of content should point the audience to the next step, whether that's visiting the website, making a booking, downloading a guide, or signing up for updates. A clear CTA helps convert engagement into action and keeps your audience moving deeper into your brand experience—and ideally, back to your website, where conversions can happen.

And Consider These for Your Personal Brand Assessment:

14. **Create and Share Blog Posts and Thought Leadership Content:** Consistently publishing high-quality blog posts or articles that showcase expertise can boost SEO, drive organic traffic, and position you as a trusted authority in your industry.

15. **Prep to Guest on Relevant Podcasts or Broadcast Interviews:** Share thought leadership in engaging conversations that have a "shelf-life" and constant presence on digital platforms to promote yourself or your company and brand.

16. **Host or Participate in Webinars and Online Events:** These not only increase your brand's visibility but also provide opportunities for back-linking and thought leadership

17. **Network, Attend, or Speak at Conferences:** This will increase visibility among the specific audiences with whom you wish to connect.

Marketing Mantras

In this chapter, we explored how physical and digital visibility work together to enhance brand engagement. Whether it's through sensory branding, creative activations, or digital campaigns, successful marketing requires a holistic approach that integrates both realms. These mantras reflect the importance of creating cohesive, memorable experiences that align both physical and digital marketing efforts with customer expectations and behaviors.

1. **Blend the Physical and Digital Presence with AI:** Marketing success lies in seamlessly integrating physical and digital strategies, further enhanced by AI technologies. Ensure clear outdoor signage and optimize digital presence with geo-targeted campaigns and AI-driven personalization to enhance visibility and engagement.

2. **Leverage the Experiential Marketing 7Es Framework:** Dr. Batat's 7Es (experience, exchange, extension, emphasis, empathy, emotional touchpoints, and emic/etic process) offer a powerful toolkit for customer-centered marketing strategies that build deeper emotional connections across physical and digital touchpoints.

3. **Address Awareness Gaps First:** Awareness, not misconceptions, often hinders success. For example, the lack of visibility for hotel restaurants or donut shops stems more from restricted physical marketing and digital outreach than from public bias. Identify and address such gaps for impactful campaigns.

4. **Create Rich Media Content:** Engage audiences with high-quality visuals, interactive content, and videos that evoke emotions and make brands memorable. Rich media is a must-have today.

5. **Drive Traffic to Digital Platforms (Part A and Part B):** A website update is only the starting point (Part A). Part B—strategically driving traffic to the website through paid ads, organic SEO, email marketing, and landing pages—is equally critical to convert updates into actionable results. (Similarly, remember to have your LinkedIn page optimized before you send a resume, because the potential employer is likely to take a first look at that page.)

6. **Use Sensory Branding for Physical Presence:** Enhance physical visibility through sensory experiences. Whether it's emitting the smell of fresh donuts onto the street or curating a unique soundscape for a café, sensory elements draw attention and strengthen brand identity.

7. **Implement Localized Marketing:** Engage local communities through strategies like geo-targeted campaigns, pop-up events, or partnerships with

neighborhood schools and businesses. These efforts build loyalty and drive foot traffic.

8. **Conduct a Digital Audit:** Analyze and enhance a brand's digital presence by reviewing SEO, website functionality, paid search, social media engagement, and online reviews. This comprehensive assessment identifies opportunities for greater visibility and improved customer experience. *There are other digital elements depending upon your role, goals, or other marketing priorities. What's shared here are the basics. Develop your own checklist for future assessments.*

9. **Adapt to Customer Behavior and Technology:** Stay responsive to emerging technologies, like QR codes, which streamline customer journeys and meet modern expectations for convenience. Embracing tools that enhance both physical and digital interactions is crucial for staying competitive.

10. **Ask yourself:** Is your brand visible enough, physically and digitally? Consider conducting a self-audit to identify gaps and opportunities in your marketing to meet your intended goals.

# # #

In this chapter, we explored the vital interplay between physical and digital visibility, highlighting how brands can enhance customer engagement through a cohesive approach. By integrating sensory branding and leveraging digital strategies, businesses can create memorable experiences that resonate with audiences. As we transition to the next chapter, we'll explore the power of presentation—drawing insights from TED Talks and sharing practical tips to boost confidence, refine content, and effectively present marketing recommendations to connect with customers.

Marketing Mindset in Motion

If your brand isn't seen, it isn't chosen. Imagine you are assessing a business's visibility, both physically and digitally. Walk through their storefront, their website, and their social media presence. Is the brand easy to find? Is the messaging clear and compelling? Or is this a brand of mystery and exclusivity that deliberately does not want to be found so easily? How does that work?

Now, think about your professional or personal brand. How visible are you? What simple steps could you take today to enhance both your physical and digital presence?

6

The Power of the Presentation

In the journey of mastering marketing and effective communication, each foundational element—whether it's knowing your why, understanding the brand, identifying marketing goals, building relationships and trust, or applying technical skills like research and persona creation—serves as a critical building block. "The Power of the Presentation" chapter seamlessly bridges these core principles with the essential skill of effectively communicating your ideas and strategies.

Just as understanding your brand and building trust lay the groundwork for successful marketing and communication initiatives, the ability to present these initiatives with clarity, passion, and authenticity ensures they resonate and drive action. By linking the strategic insights from previous chapters with robust presentation techniques, this chapter tells us of the importance of crafting compelling marketing plans and delivering them in a way that inspires and engages the audience. This interconnected approach empowers marketers to design impactful strategies and effectively share and implement them, fostering stronger client relationships to achieve greater marketing success.

Presentation is more than just delivering a set of slides or pitching an idea. It's a crucial opportunity to reflect both your expertise and professionalism. When marketing to clients, how you present yourself is just as important as the recommendations you share. In class, I always stress that balancing directness with sensitivity is key; you want to address challenges openly while maintaining respect and a positive, forward-moving tone. This approach builds rapport and ensures your message resonates and drives meaningful action. It also demonstrates that you are part of the team; *remember "we" rather than "you."*

In this chapter, I share several of the practical strategies and techniques I have taught over the years to enhance presentation skills, strengthen client connections, and communicate marketing recommendations and insights effectively. By focusing on clear communication, genuine engagement, and confidence (with humility, not arrogance) in your delivery, you'll be better equipped to gain trust and inspire buy-in while delivering your researched and evidence-based marketing suggestions.

Who is TED? TED—technology, entertainment, and design—is a global platform that champions the "power of ideas." Through concise, impactful talks, TED brings together leading thinkers, innovators, and storytellers from around the world, showcasing a wide variety of perspectives. These talks have become a cultural phenomenon, shared online and viewed by millions, because they exemplify how compelling communication can spark inspiration, foster learning, and encourage new ways of thinking.

What makes TED significant is not just its breadth of topics but how the speakers deliver their messages. Each talk is distilled to its most essential insights, supported by engaging anecdotes and visuals, and delivered with clarity and authenticity. This style teaches us valuable lessons about presenting new information to any audience: keep your message focused, connect emotionally through storytelling, and ensure every visual element adds to the narrative. By learning from TED speakers, we can refine our presentation skills to resonate powerfully and stick with listeners long after we've left the stage.

Each semester, I require students to read a practical professional-development book, *Talk Like TED* by Carmine Gallo. It is not a textbook. I find Gallo's easy-to-comprehend writing and his deep dive into the world of TED talks immensely valuable for honing presentation skills. Carmine Gallo is a respected communication coach and keynote speaker who has extensively researched the techniques behind successful

TED presenters. Each August, I reread the first three chapters of *Talk Like TED* to continually prepare myself for the upcoming academic year. By integrating Gallo's successful TED talk insights—from storytelling to engaging visuals and authentic delivery—our students are far better prepared to craft compelling marketing plan presentations.

TED Practices

So, what are the nine commonalities that Gallo has uncovered in the TED talks he's analyzed? What makes for an effective talk? Here are the nine presentation tips Gallo spells out in his engaging book.

1. **Deliver your insight with passion.** Passionate delivery turns a presentation into an engaging experience. When you speak with genuine enthusiasm, your energy draws the audience in and inspires them to care about your message. In the case of connecting with your client, passion demonstrates that you care about their business and that you consider yourself part of their team.

   "From my project (an app for Boston area events), I learned to appeal to emotions when presenting to somebody, especially if it is about their business, and I want to connect more deeply with that person. Yes, content, research, and creativity are indeed important, but what people truly remember is how you

made them feel." Richard Peet Hannah, BU School of Hospitality, Class of 2022

2. **Master the art of storytelling.** Connect with your audience (or client). Storytelling is a powerful tool that enables connection on a personal level. Stories evoke emotions, making your message more relatable, impactful and memorable, helping your audience retain the information long after the presentation ends.

The STR (Smith Travel Research) student competition involves university teams analyzing market data about global destinations to share a synopsis of trends, observations, and potential possibilities for hospitality growth. Paulina, one of my "sensational six" teaching assistants at BU, participated in a STR competition and shares this bit of advice:

"For the STR competition, our team needed to analyze data to tell the hospitality development story about two specific global markets: Washington, DC, and Tokyo, Japan. I was clueless. I had no idea how to create that story. But thanks to our primary resources and the interviews and questions we asked of industry experts, we had a clearer view of the interpretation of the data. We ultimately learned about the significance of gastronomy and culinary experiences in Tokyo. That led us to start our presentation with a video of Japan's most famous chef sharing his country's

unique food history. It set the tone for our audience to enjoy the rest of our information and learn from our storytelling techniques. The reception we received from the audiences and the judges was enthusiastic, thanks to our varied way of conveying what could be perceived as 'dry' information." Paulina Preciat, BU School of Hospitality, Class of 2023

# # #

"Videos are an effective vehicle for storytelling. I loved that we made videos as part of our class projects in our digital marketing course. This experience was important. We learned that the videos did not need to be professionally produced. Rather, the raw and authentic videos on an iPhone, depending on the story, can prove even better, especially for short-form messaging.

"It's easy. Take an iPhone, use a gimbal (stabilizer), and film. You can produce nice content. The power of video for brand storytelling cannot be underestimated. Retrieve 'success statistics' from HubSpot and measure engagement, too.

"One should always be thinking, Is this better as a video? *Videos today should be under two minutes. Short-form videos are extremely effective for digital visibility."* Elise Borkan Mackin, BU School of Hospitality, Class of 2019

3. **Have a conversation.** Speaking in a conversational tone invites participation, breaks barriers, and keeps your message relatable. With clients, treat recommendations as two-way discussions to foster connection and build buy-in.

   I tell students that while sharing our marketing recommendations is their "final presentation," we will be sitting around the same table as our clients and engaging them in conversation, which will elicit camaraderie, connection, and openness to our researched ideas.

4. **Teach people something new.** Introducing fresh ideas or perspectives keeps your audience engaged and curious. When people learn something novel, it triggers their interest and encourages them to think differently, leaving a lasting impression. Teaching new concepts also positions you as a thought leader, enhancing your credibility.

"The concept of always teaching your audience something new felt like a revelation when I first heard it in class. It has been immensely useful and enlightening in my profession since graduation.

"Currently, I am working on a startup related to technology-assisted wellness. My goal is to raise awareness about the importance of early rehabilitation and wellness, using technology and scientific

methods to achieve better results than traditional medication or supplements.

"My clients are especially engaged when I explain the strong government support for this industry and the reasoning behind our products. These are long-standing challenges that have affected countless people and families for decades, and we are providing innovative solutions through technology and artificial intelligence." Tianyuan (Judy) Zhang, BU School of Hospitality, Class of 2023

5. **Deliver jaw-dropping moments.** Surprising your audience with unexpected facts, demonstrations, or revelations can create a lasting impact. These "wow" moments capture attention and leave a strong impression. By breaking the norm, you can spark curiosity and excitement, keeping your audience on the edge of their seats.

   One of our class's favorite jaw-dropping moments in a TED is that delivered by Bill Gates (2009, "Malaria, Mosquitos, and Education") in which Gates informs about the perils of malaria and the necessity of vaccines with an impactful gesture. As he's talking about mosquitoes, he opens a jar, releasing them into the audience to a loud gasp of fright. It's memorable, it's a "wow" moment, and Gates made his point.

6. **Lighten up.** Incorporating humor or light-hearted moments can make your presentation more

enjoyable and relatable. Laughter or a lightened atmosphere fosters a positive connection, ensuring your presentation is both impactful and memorable.

When our students deliver marketing recommendations to comedy clubs or college-oriented restaurants, the lightened mood is certainly fitting. If the marketing is to help a destination, let's say Boston, during the pandemic, knowing when it's appropriate to "let go" or "share something funny" is an art that must be practiced. We must be careful with humor; we never want to offend anyone.

7. **Stick to the eighteen-minute rule.** Keeping the presentation concise ensures that your audience remains focused and engaged. The eighteen-minute rule forces us to distill the message to its essence, delivering only the most important points. This brevity respects your audience's time and prevents information overload.

   As a side note, when we present in class to clients, our first rehearsal is typically forty-five minutes. During our second rehearsal in class, the dress rehearsal, we condense the presentation to approximately thirty minutes by editing content and practicing continuously to deliver the information seamlessly and confidently. By the time we deliver our final presentation to the client in class, it typically ranges from eighteen to twenty-four minutes. Just the right amount of time to keep the client's attention and share critical content to encourage Q&A.

8. **Paint a mental picture with multi-sensory experiences.** Engaging multiple senses helps the audience vividly visualize and experience the message. By using descriptive language, visual aids, and even sound, we can create a rich, immersive experience that stays with our audience.

   For our Newsfeed Café marketing recommendations, the students brought in a boombox to play jazz music to start the presentation; for Union Square Donuts, the students brought in a smell machine (yes, there is such a thing) to blast the scent of baked goods. Help your audience or client paint that mental picture with creative sensory accessories.

9. **Stay in your lane.** Focusing on your area of expertise ensures that you speak with authority and confidence. When you stay within your realm of knowledge, you can provide depth and insight, which enhances your credibility. Trying to cover too much or venturing into areas outside your expertise can dilute your message and weaken the overall impact of your presentation. This is also why research is critical to the presentation. The more familiar you are with your topic and recommendations, the easier it is to deliver the information, because you know it. You got this!

I often find myself straying from my lane because I want to share too much tangential information. I love sharing additional knowledge and telling stories, but this often takes me off topic, wastes everyone's valuable time, and makes me appear unfocused or scatter-brained. Don't fall into my trap, though I may have done that throughout these pages. Apologies.

Leora's Additional Presentation Tips

In my semesters of teaching this fabulous advanced Experiential Marketing course, I have also collected additional best practices to share with students. Allow me to add a few more thoughts to Gallo and TED:

1. **More is not More:** Overloading a presentation with details can overwhelm your audience and dilute your message. Focus on the essentials to make key points clearer, more memorable, and more impactful. A streamlined approach also invites curiosity and deeper engagement. Clarity and conciseness amplify the power of what you're trying to say.

   I would add that for the presentation slides as well, less is more. The less content on a slide, the easier the read, and the more memorable. If you are sharing a data point, just show the number on the slide. If showing a person or character, use only the image. The more striking the slide, thanks to less content, the more intriguing the presentation.

2. **Pattern of Three:** The pattern of three has long been a powerhouse in effective communication. For example, think of phrases like "Stop, drop, and roll," "Lights, camera, action," or even "I came, I saw, I conquered." By grouping information, instructions, or ideas into three concise parts, you create a memorable rhythm and make it far easier for your audience to recall and repeat your message. This principle works just as well in writing as it does in speech because it naturally lends structure and clarity. Whether you're trying to persuade a client, rally a team, or inspire a crowd (see what I did here?), delivering your points in three ensures your words stand out and stick.

"When speaking, share only the three most important points. This is a principle I've been using since the day I heard it in our marketing class. As an audience member, I find it easier to remember and reflect on information presented in this format. As a presenter or even in daily life during meetings with my supervisor or clients, this structure helps me formulate my thoughts with clarity in my mind. You sound more logical when you answer a question knowing your first, second, and third points." Mingjing He, BU School of Hospitality, Class of 2019

3. **Bookending:** Bookending is a powerful technique that involves starting with a story or memorable idea, then returning to it at the conclusion of your presentation or written piece. Repeating a key idea at the beginning and end reinforces its importance and creates a cohesive, memorable narrative. From a mnemonic standpoint, this approach helps listeners or readers mentally link new information back to the initial concept, making it easier to recall your recommendations or content long after the conversation has ended.

   I've at times played Billy Joel's "Scenes from an Italian Restaurant" in class—all seven minutes and thirty-seven seconds of it. This is a beautiful example of using the bookending technique in his storytelling. Billy starts with the story of a couple who meet at a restaurant and reminisces about "the old days." Then he shares the stories they are recalling and finally concludes by circling back to the couple in the restaurant. It's a long song to play in class—but I don't care. It's a great song.

   Or just put your arms out as if you're going to hug someone. That's "bookending" them; you've just wrapped your arms around them. That's what this technique does for a presentation. It's wrapping the gift.

4. **Everyone's Prepared:** Know all the material, not just your parts. Another important tip is ensuring

that *everyone* on the team is ready to present, no matter the circumstances. Life happens, and people get sick or other emergencies arise, and when a presenter is suddenly unavailable, the rest of the team should be able to seamlessly deliver the full presentation. I've encountered this scenario in my classes more than once, and the projects that truly succeed are those in which each team member is prepared to cover any section of the content at a moment's notice. Not only does this readiness create a smoother, more professional experience for clients or audiences, but it also demonstrates a high level of collaboration and commitment from the entire team.

I remember, back in fifth grade (1975!), my class performed a Disney song in front of the whole school. At the last minute, I realized a classmate of mine (though I don't remember who), the soloist, didn't show up. Even though I was far from a trained singer (and honestly still don't know what compelled me), I stepped up and sang her line. Incredibly, the show went on seamlessly, and no one in the audience even realized anything was amiss. That unexpected moment taught me how crucial it is for every team member to be prepared to fill in, no matter the circumstances. Whether it's a school performance or a marketing pitch, having everyone ready ensures the presentation never misses a beat and underscores the team's adaptability and professionalism.

5. **Zoom Readiness:** Knowing how to present effectively on Zoom is an essential skill in today's professional landscape. From your environment and attire, what the camera actually sees and hears, to the way you project energy through the screen, every detail contributes to how your message is received.

- Keep your camera on to foster a sense of connection and look directly at the lens when speaking to simulate eye contact. Actively acknowledge teammates and audience members through smiles, nods, and verbal affirmations. To combat audience fatigue, vary your speaking pace and incorporate brief interactive segments. (*Forbes* reports that presentations incorporating interactive elements see a 20 percent increase in audience engagement compared to those that do not.)

- If you're concerned about distractions behind you, blur your background, and always include a clear name plate so clients or colleagues know who you are.

- Avoid cluttering slides with too much text. Incorporate multimedia elements like short videos or animations to illustrate key points and maintain audience interest. HubSpot highlights that presentations with visually engaging content are 43 percent more likely to hold the audience's attention.

- Leverage Zoom's interactive tools to enhance engagement and participation. Incorporate polls to gather instant feedback and keep the audience involved. Use the Q&A feature to address questions in real-time, fostering a two-way dialogue. Breakout rooms can facilitate smaller group discussions, encouraging collaboration and deeper interaction.

These techniques will help bring depth and professionalism to an otherwise "flat" platform, ensuring the audience remains engaged and confident in your expertise.

Yet, technical difficulties can disrupt the flow of a Zoom presentation and detract from your professionalism. To minimize these risks, ensure there is a reliable internet connection and familiarize yourself with Zoom's features. Conduct a tech check with your team to troubleshoot potential issues with audio, video, and screen sharing. A backup device or a secondary internet source can provide a safety net in case of unexpected disruptions.

The point of these tips is to elevate Zoom presentations from mere video calls to powerful, engaging experiences.

6. **Stay Informed—Always:** One of the simplest yet most impactful habits you can adopt is to follow your client on social media, regularly check their website, and keep tabs on competitor

activity. This real-time monitoring ensures you're up to date on any last-minute changes or breaking news—even on the morning of your presentation. I've seen client websites get revamped just hours before a student marketing presentation, and acknowledging these changes in real-time earns trust and respect. Likewise, pending legislation, like the one affecting our Rooted In (cannabis dispensary) client, needs to be top of mind so you can speak to it proactively. By staying informed, you earn trust and gain respect.

7. **Rehearse. Practice. Rehearse and Practice Some More:** Practice is the engine that drives a successful presentation. Even the most compelling ideas can fall flat without careful rehearsal to iron out kinks in delivery, pacing, and transitions. By running through your material multiple times, you build confidence, identify weak spots, and perfect the flow—ensuring that both you and your team come across as polished, cohesive, and ready to engage any audience.

   To maximize the effectiveness of rehearsals, incorporate specific techniques, such as practicing in front of a mirror to observe your body language, recording yourself to evaluate tone and pacing, and conducting mock presentations with peers to simulate real-world scenarios. Additionally, rehearse while wearing the attire you plan to wear for the actual presentation to become comfortable and ensure it doesn't hinder your movements or delivery.

Regular practice not only reduces anxiety but also improves the overall delivery and equips us to handle unexpected questions with confidence. Whether practicing alone, with friends, or with our team, consistent rehearsal ensures we are thoroughly prepared to present the marketing plan recommendations seamlessly and professionally.

Recollections and Reflections

"Keep it concise. You have a limited period of attention from the audience, so it must be used wisely. In that regard, always ask yourself if there is a better way to articulate a point. Is there a stronger title, a better word or phrase to pique curiosity, or a "wow moment" that my audience will always remember? "Practice, practice, practice. The effort shows. Practice improves everything. It all comes down to confidence. If you are not confident, you are not going to present comfortably. Practice is the best tool to gain confidence.

"I had a personal challenge that attests to this. When I was selected to deliver a TEDx on campus, I could only think of how challenging it would be to deliver the speech. Thankfully, it was during the semester when I took the Strategic Marketing class, and one of my favorite lessons from that class was to practice and practice more. I took that same approach for the TEDx, and I can honestly say

that I never felt more confident than when I was giving that talk.

"I would also recommend that you prepare a presentation that answers all the questions that your client might ask. There was a particular presentation I delivered for a job, and I received favorable feedback. One individual said to me, 'Your presentation really answered most of the questions I had from the start, and that was terrific.'" Paulina Preciat, BU School of Hospitality Administration, Class of 2023.

# # #

"During my senior year, in the Advanced Marketing class, I was part of a team tasked with creating a full-scale marketing plan for the Del Frisco's Steakhouse in the Seaport District of Boston. The resulting comprehensive plan consisted of a competitive analysis, identification of the target audiences, research to understand the restaurant's positioning for each market, creative promotional recommendations, and some operational ideas, too.

"Preparing the plan was half the challenge. Presenting in front of your client, in this case, the company's director of operations, was equally challenging. We had to be prepared for any question that came our way. I learned valuable presentation skills that I still use today when I present PR plans to my clients, such as not reading directly off PowerPoints, the ability to speak to my teammates'

sections should they be absent, and the skill of presenting an abundance of information to the client in an easy, digestible way. And of course, acknowledging or congratulating the client regarding the successful and positive aspects of their business while delicately suggesting opportunities to take existing processes to new directions. As important as that fifty-four-page marketing plan was, the actual presentation of our information to the client greatly impacted our success and relationship." Ally Rung, BU School of Hospitality, Class of 2017

Both Ally and Paulina highlight the critical importance of authenticity and emotional engagement in presentations. Ally emphasizes the value of conveying information clearly and concisely while remaining adaptable to ensure seamless delivery, even in unexpected situations. Paulina talks about the power of storytelling and the use of genuine, relatable content to connect with the audience. Together, their experiences demonstrate that effective presentations are built on a foundation of thorough preparation.

Marketing Mantras

It's essential to recognize that the power of a presentation lies in the content we deliver and how we present it. Effective communication is a harmonious blend of compelling content, passionate delivery, storytelling, the pattern of three, wow moments, and ensuring that our message leaves a lasting impression.

1. **Embrace Storytelling to Forge Emotional Connections:** Using narratives transforms abstract concepts into relatable and memorable experiences. By weaving compelling stories into presentations, we engage our audience on a personal level, making the message more impactful and resonating long after the presentation concludes.

2. **Prioritize Clarity and Conciseness:** By streamlining our presentation to focus on the most critical points, we enhance clarity and keep the audience engaged. "Less is more" helps us prevent information overload and ensures our key messages are memorable and easily digestible.

3. **Foster Team Preparedness and Flexibility:** When every team member is well-prepared and capable of handling any part of the presentation, it promotes professionalism and adaptability. This readiness not only guarantees a seamless delivery but also demonstrates a united and competent team, building greater trust with your audience.

4. **Leverage Visuals and Multimedia Effectively:** Incorporating visuals and short-form videos can significantly enhance your storytelling and keep your audience engaged.

5. **Cultivate Authenticity and Passion in Delivery:** Presenting with genuine enthusiasm and sincerity fosters a deeper connection with your audience. Authenticity and passion demonstrate

your commitment to the subject matter, inspiring trust and encouraging your audience to invest emotionally in your message. Convey your sense of style and be who you are, not someone else. An audience is most receptive when you speak from the heart.

\# \# \#

Effective communication hinges on the seamless integration of compelling content, passionate delivery, and engaging storytelling. By embracing these key strategies—fostering emotional connections, prioritizing clarity, preparing our teams, leveraging visuals, and cultivating authenticity—we can create memorable presentations that have lasting impacts. In the next chapter, we will explore the significance of marketing and meaningful partnerships, focusing on how these elements can further strengthen our connections with audiences.

Marketing Mindset in Motion

Think about the most compelling presentation you've ever seen. What made it memorable? Was it the storytelling, the clarity, or the delivery? Now, reflect on your presentation style. How can you apply techniques like the pattern of three, bookending, or TED-style engagement to ensure your next presentation leaves a lasting impact?

7

Conscious Marketing and Impactful Partnerships

Since I began teaching the Experiential Marketing (formerly called Advanced Strategic Marketing) course in the fall of 2015, I have required students to incorporate a CSR (corporate social responsibility) initiative as part of the marketing recommendations. As we helped owners drive revenue through effective marketing, it was just as important to ensure every business and marketing initiative positively impacted people, place, and planet.

It's one thing to be conscious, but it's something else entirely to act meaningfully on that consciousness. I encourage businesses to *intentionally create positive impact and communicate it effectively to achieve success.*

Conscious Marketing

I would add that conscious marketing (CM) goes beyond profit-driven strategies by centering on values such as empathy, honesty, and social responsibility. At its heart, it is a purpose-driven approach, with marketing guided by meaningful goals beyond just sales—focusing on positive social, environmental, or cultural impact. CM seeks to create genuine connections, empower consumers, and foster positive change for society, the environment, and businesses themselves. Initiatives might address issues such as:

- **Consumer Welfare and Empowerment:** Ensure consumers' well-being by providing accurate information, fair practices, and respecting privacy.

- **Social and Environmental Responsibility:** Commit to sustainability, support social causes, and minimize environmental impact to protect communities, ecosystems, and cultural heritage. This embraces the brand's role in community and culture impact, ensuring marketing efforts contribute positively to the places and people they touch.

- **Transparency and Accountability:** Share product and operational details openly, admit mistakes, and take corrective action to build trust and credibility.

- **Fairness and Inclusivity:** Promote fairness in hiring, advertising, and customer service while respecting cultural richness and avoiding stereotypes.

- **Authenticity and Brand Purpose:** Align actions with core values, communicate with empathy, and let purpose-driven decisions foster consumer trust.

- **Continuous Improvement and Leadership:** Treat ethical marketing as an ongoing commitment, seek feedback, refine strategies, and set high industry standards.

- **Collaboration and Community Engagement:** Partner with communities, support local initiatives, and use your brand's platform to advocate for shared goals that strengthen cultural ties and promote growth for all.

Let's focus on this final point: Forming partnerships that go beyond profit to create positive impact for all stakeholders is another marketing approach businesses should consider. It's about spreading the genuine joy of doing good for others—people, place, or planet.

Building Trust

In the March 2024 *Marketing SmartBrief* article, "Ethical Marketing: Building Trust and Consumer Engagement in the Digital Age," the authors highlight that ethical and sustainable marketing has become essential for brands looking to forge genuine connections with increasingly conscientious consumers. This shift spans multiple generations—from Baby Boomers to Gen Z—who now demand more information and accountability from the brands they choose to support.

- Ethical marketing and environmentally responsible practices anchor strong, enduring relationships with today's perceptive and well-informed customers. For instance, the 2023 Business of Sustainability Index (PDI Technologies) indicates that 68 percent of American consumers are willing to pay a premium for products deemed environmentally sustainable.

- Conscious consumers, as highlighted in the article, go beyond a product's basic appeal by examining whether a brand adopts ethical methods, ranging from sustainability initiatives to corporate social responsibility. They conduct their research with the help of platforms such as Good On You, Cruelty-Free Kitty, and Ethical Elephant, which rate brands on factors such as eco-friendly sourcing and potential animal cruelty. This development is prompting brands to align their core values with those of their customers. As the *Marketing SmartBrief* piece noted, businesses looking to remain relevant in crowded markets must prioritize ethical marketing if they hope to satisfy the growing demand for honesty and openness.

- A commitment to trust and authenticity is core to ethical marketing. Much like influencers who substantiate their claims through genuine engagement and demonstrable impact, brands must clearly show how they fulfill ethical standards. Consumers today, inundated by data and online information, are more skeptical than ever; they want evidence that a brand's promises are genuine before devoting their money and loyalty.

The same article details several foundational principles essential for ethical marketing. When companies openly communicate their sourcing practices, own up to mistakes, and acknowledge their influence on both society and the environment, they are more likely to gain consumer trust, thereby setting the stage for meaningful, long-term customer relationships.

Corporate Social Responsibility (CSR)

When we think and act as conscious marketers, we embrace a framework that prioritizes responsibility and accountability. This means carefully considering the human and environmental consequences of our marketing efforts. It's about more than just promoting a product or service; it's about ensuring that our actions contribute positively to people and places. In the hospitality industry, this could translate into initiatives that benefit local communities, support sustainable tourism, or reduce environmental footprints.

This responsibility extends to every aspect of our business, from the products we promote to the way we interact with our customers and stakeholders. As hospitality professionals, we have the power to influence and inspire change. Whether through eco-friendly practices, community engagement, or promoting cultural heritage, our marketing efforts can create a meaningful difference.

The hospitality industry holds a unique responsibility to contribute positively to society by enhancing people's well-being, embodying the true essence of hospitality, which centers on how individuals feel. By encouraging hospitality businesses to move beyond providing services and to extend their efforts in meaningful ways, we can collectively work toward creating a better and more compassionate world.

This emphasis on CSR has always been paramount to me. In recent years, my perspective has been profoundly shaped by witnessing the adverse and alarming effects of climate change on my international travels, as well as experiencing travel disruptions due to health crises affecting loved ones. These experiences have reinforced my commitment to ensuring that all our marketing efforts in hospitality (at least from my classroom) are firmly rooted in CSR.

#   #   #

"I remember discussing the topic of conscious marketing when working on a team project for Motto by Hilton, a hotel concept that centers around immersing guests in local culture. With such a strong focus on locality, it was important that we incorporate conscious marketing into our campaign.

> *"Our team devised a clothing drive initiative in collaboration with a local service organization that would encourage employee and neighborhood engagement while giving back to the local community. The aim of adding conscious marketing to our campaign was not to create a false or vast sense of charity but to incorporate a real and effective initiative that would have an impact on a specific, local community. Conscious marketing is significantly more important with younger generations supporting brands that share their same values. Companies can no longer hide behind vague sustainability statements because Gen Z performs their due diligence. Conscious marketing should be present, and it must also be authentic."* Hoda Sherdy, BU School of Hospitality, Class of 2021

Classroom Cases

In an age of increasing consumer awareness and social consciousness, marketers are called to prioritize ethics, responsibility, and acting with integrity in their practices. How can businesses align their marketing strategies with ethical values, social responsibility, and the greater good?

Sometimes, it takes an outside perspective to spot opportunities. That's what our class does when we "search the forest through the trees," identifying brand-aligned partnerships and causes that enable companies to do good -- even if they already think they are. Several of our classroom projects advanced our goal and contributed to the well-being of our community. In these projects, the students truly shone.

I. **Community Cooks: Innovating Volunteer Engagement for Nonprofit Success**

Overview: In the spring of 2019, Daniele Levine, executive director of Community Cooks (CC) asked our students to consider the following information and challenges: Founded in 1990, Community Cooks is a nonprofit based in Somerville, Massachusetts, that mobilizes individuals, businesses, civic, educational, and faith-based groups to provide home-prepared food for vulnerable populations who seek assistance from human service agencies. By providing free home-cooked meals, CC seeks to: build a bridge of caring between volunteers and neighbors in need, help partner agencies stretch limited resources so they can focus on delivering critical services, and send a message of caring, comfort, and dignity to our meal beneficiaries along with physical nourishment. At the time, CC was over 900 volunteers strong, providing meals to more than 4,600 neighbors in need each month in communities throughout Greater Boston.

Situation Analysis: Community Cooks was founded as an all-volunteer organization in 2012 and became a 501(c)(3) nonprofit. In just over six years (spring 2019), CC had grown substantially, more than tripling in size and impact and more than doubling the annual budget.

As Community Cooks grew to find their new normal in the aftermath of the founder's retirement in 2018, the organization was continually looking for the most effective ways to retain and grow its donor base to support a recently expanded budget, *and* seeking strategies to retain, nurture, and grow its community of volunteers. The two groups often overlap but sometimes require different approaches. They communicated with supporters via social media, e-blasts, e-newsletters, limited written collateral, and their website, which at the time was very outdated and in need of an overhaul. CC wanted to maintain the personal, "small town" community identity that "makes us unique" while professionalizing for growth. Their question was, "What can we do now to tackle our marketing and messaging challenges, given that we have a limited budget and a staff of four who are already stretched?"

Marketing Challenges: The students were asked: "How do we effectively communicate our impact and highlight what makes our model unique, in a way that engages donors, moves them, and encourages them to invest in Community Cooks? Given limited time and money, what is the best place to invest our resources right now and how?"

The students were also tasked with addressing this challenge: "How can we most effectively communicate with our volunteer cooks -- including individuals, businesses and faith-based and educational groups, so they feel connected to our community, engaged, and motivated to sustain their commitment over time?"

Student Recommendations: This was a case of the organization operating as a CSR-focused entity. The students were tasked with assessing and strategically streamlining existing marketing activities to ensure all work was manageable and cohesive. Suggestions included redesigning and rethinking the volunteer newsletter content; introducing new ways to recognize and reward volunteers and groups, such as attendance at gala events or receiving thank-you cookbooks; planning for the annual fundraising gala more sustainably; and maintaining communication with individual and group volunteers. Volunteer engagement, relationships, and loyalty are critical to the success of this socially important organization.

Feedback: Daniele attentively listened to the students and graciously welcomed many of the communication recommendations. She particularly embraced the reward and recognition element, recognizing it as a vital role in fostering volunteerism, which is essential to the organization's success.

II. Marriott Long Wharf: Protecting the Harbor While Renovating Itself

Overview: Former Marriott Long Wharf General Manager Ed Rocco has always been an amazing friend to my classes and our hospitality students. In the fall of 2017, he approached our class with the following situation: this hotel was about to undergo a large-scale renovation, and we needed to inform prospective guests. Within walking distance of Boston's Historic Long Wharf Pier and tourist attractions like Faneuil Hall Marketplace and the Freedom Trail, the Marriott Long Wharf is a prime harborside location. Its elegant accommodations serve all types of travelers, from business executives to families, and its event spaces – capable of hosting up to 850 guests, offer versatile options for any occasion.

Situation Analysis: In 2018, the hotel embarked on its extensive room renovation; the hotel owner, California-based Sunstone, invested approximately $40 million in capital improvements. Guest rooms were gutted to studs, and double-doubles were converted to double-queens (bedded rooms). Bathrooms were expanded by two feet, and bathtubs were replaced with spa showers. The total per-key cost was approximately $72,000.

In addition to the guest rooms, the hotel constructed a new bi-level M Club Lounge complete with a glass elevator. The restaurant saw a more modest renovation with expanded seating and a new back bar, opening the harbor views for guests to enjoy. The library was expanded to the current business center. The new business center was relocated to the front seating area of the concierge desk.

At the time, in preparation for this total hotel renovation, a marketing plan covering several key areas was critical to successfully repositioning the hotel.

Marketing Challenge A): Create a multi-faceted social media plan targeting group, BT (business transient), and leisure segments. How do we communicate our repositioning plan from a pre-renovation standpoint through renovation and then post-renovation via social media, collateral, and proactive communications?

Marketing Challenge B): The Boston Marriott Long Wharf utilizes OTA (online travel agency) booking sites (Expedia, Booking.com) to sell room nights. "Please research how other luxury hotels are positioned on these channels, including imagery, copy, amenities, and any other content that compels you to click on a hotel." What adjustments should be made to Long

Wharf's OTA sites to create a compelling story, so customers book our luxury rooms? Are there services or amenities that would compel you to book at this high rate? Present your assessment in the format of an OTA marketing plan.

Student Recommendations: The team conducted Qualtrics surveys to determine that the unique selling proposition (USP) of the hotel is its wonderful waterfront location. Survey results were very telling: Consumers affirmed that corporate social responsibility and any opportunity to maintain and improve the waterfront and Boston Harbor are important. When A/B testing photography, it was also evident that imagery of the harbor and the waterfront was important for social media appeal, digital platforms, and the OTA sites. Because the hotel was renovated and repositioned to more of a lifestyle hotel, survey respondents noted that the harbor front images projected an aspirational lifestyle that they desired when traveling, even for business.

The students delved deeper into the CSR initiatives and potential partnerships. Through their research, they found that 87 percent of respondents felt it was moderately, very, or extremely important for a hotel company to take responsibility for its effects on the environment and social well-being. Furthermore, chart from a Huffington Post article at the time demonstrated how important CSR was to Millennials specifically. Over 83 percent of Millennials believed that businesses should be involved in societal issues, equaling the responses received in the student survey.

Since the students' proposed repositioning campaign slogan for the hotel was "Make a Splash," which capitalized on the waterfront benefit, the team recommended a partnership with Save the Harbor/Save the Bay. This organization is comprised of thousands of citizens, civic, corporate, cultural, and community leaders, and scientists with a mission to restore and protect Boston Harbor and Massachusetts Bay for the public to enjoy.

My students strongly encouraged the hotel to position itself as a community leader in the harbor area. This partnership would include the opportunity for hotel employees to volunteer on beach cleanup days or aid in other initiatives of Save the Harbor.

The student team shared another suggestion: working with Save the Harbor for the National Humanities Conference, which was held at the Hyatt Regency Boston in the past. The conference featured speakers, meetings, and tours of the harbor and surrounding historical areas.

To communicate this partnership to consumers, students suggested a dedicated tab on the website, giving potential customers easy access to the hotel's CSR initiatives. Additionally, an amenity would be offered to guests, to promote both the Save the Harbor's community work. This upon-arrival gift -- designed to encourage consumers to "Make a Splash" or "Dive Into" saving the Boston Harbor -- could contain a sleep mask, lotion, lip balm, and a sea salt scrub, all featuring printed images of fish to help create excitement for the organization.

Students also suggested a partnership with nearby Harpoon Brewery, which was known for its efforts to reduce water and energy waste through beer production. Additionally, Harpoon Brewery had (at the time) a charitable arm dedicated to carrying out initiatives, which included donations to local charities and hosting events where proceeds went to charity as well.

Ed and his colleague Brandon Meyer listened intently as the students shared data and research to emphasize the importance of incorporating social responsibility into the DNA of the hotel offerings. Investing in philanthropic and meaningful community causes encourages guests to patronize the hotel even more. We just need to market it.

III. **Studio Allston: Strengthening Artistic Communities with Conscious Connections**

Overview and Situation Analysis: The Studio Allston hotel is a boutique hospitality experience inspired by Boston's eclectic creative community. It's not just a hotel; it's also an art gallery, with over 117 variations of one-of-a-kind in-room art and public spaces that were expertly curated by talented artists. As the hotel shares, "Come stay with us and experience life *Outside the Frame*."

Marketing Challenge: How do we best integrate the hotel more deeply into the local community? And how can we showcase inclusivity at our property?

Student Recommendations: Research led the students to develop a purpose statement for the hotel: "With its inspiring space that invokes the appreciation of art, Studio Allston is more than just a place to stay. The hotel aims to bring art into the community by showcasing local artists as if we are an art gallery. Our hotel's fundamental mission is to add color and energy to Boston with vibrant artworks and to support local artists."

Three audience personas were identified: local artists, the local community, and out-of-state travelers. Activations and opportunities were created to invite local artists to use the hotel as a platform for exhibits and studio work through "Paint and Sip Ateliers" and "Studio Allston Artist Nights." For community awareness and engagement, the paint and sip activities calendar was particularly well-received. Additional events included poetry slams, salsa dancing, classic old movie nights, and art trivia nights. These activities reflected the brand's values and reinforced its identity.

As for marketing the activities, paid and organic social media marketing, paid search, newsletter recommendations, podcasts, and partnerships with local brand-aligned organizations and representatives of the Allston Alliance were recommended to strengthen reach for mutually beneficial impact on the community.

Feedback: The hotel's regional director of sales, Efren Aponte, and social media manager, Passion Smith, are both so open to out-of-the-box thinking and ideas that the creativity of the presentation and recommendations resonated. The recommendations were so brand-aligned and spot on for the hotel; Efren and Passion continue to return to our classes for other hotels in their portfolio. Something seems to be working.

Together, these case studies highlight the practice of prioritizing sustainability, community engagement, and meaningful collaboration. Conscious marketing drives positive social and environmental outcomes and reinforces brand loyalty and long-term success.

Strategic Partnerships

Strategic partnerships are a powerful way to expand reach and connect with new audiences, but their true value lies in uniting businesses and stakeholders around a shared purpose. By pooling resources, expertise, and networks, collaborative efforts can drive positive social impact (and boost credibility) that goes beyond traditional profit motives. When organizations come together to support meaningful causes, they enhance their collective brand strength and foster lasting goodwill within the communities they serve. MMGY's EVP Julie Freeman, in our conversation for the *Boston Hospitality Review*, detailed a few of the more recent innovative marketing partnerships her agency executed for more powerful marketing reach for their client, Visit Costa Rica Tourism:

1. A series of high-profile brand partnerships, events, and activations was launched to bring Costa Rica to life in a non-traditional way and generate awareness and media buzz. Costa Rica partnered with world-renowned Cirque du Soleil as the official tourism partner in the United States for their Big Top show, "ECHO." This unique collaboration aligned perfectly with Costa Rica's *"pura vida"* way of life. The partnership included on-site activations in Atlanta and Miami from November 2023 through April 2024, original in-destination content, paid influencer promotion, and a trip giveaway. As part of the collaboration, Cirque du Soleil traveled to Costa Rica to film an episode of their Cirque RAW series, showcasing Cirque du Soleil talent in the raw and capturing the true essence and breathtaking landscapes of Costa Rica.

2. Through a first-of-its-kind partnership with Amazon and Whole Foods, Costa Rica Tourism sought to provide customers with an essential

break when they least expected it. Known for its sustainability and eco-conscious initiatives, Costa Rica is a natural fit with the Whole Foods brand, which already carries many of the country's products in its stores. This organic brand connection was the basis of a fully integrated campaign, beginning with in-store digital displays at Whole Foods that offered customers enriching facts about the country, like how five volcanoes heat hundreds of hot springs for natural relaxation.

3. Outside of stores, Volta electric-car charging station screens also featured brand messaging, showing users what a true recharge would look like for them in Costa Rica. To reach Whole Foods customers who ordered home delivery, a paper bag was designed with striking hand-drawn depictions of Costa Rica centered around a towering volcano. Drawing on the ideas of gratitude, sustainability, and enrichment, the hand-illustrated bag could be kept or given to others—reused as wrapping paper, colored and displayed, cut and collaged, or even used for ripening fruit. Costa Rica Tourism also partnered with content creators with ties to the country to amplify this message through social-first video.

4. Aiming to bring visitor numbers back to pre-pandemic levels of over 3.2 million visitors annually, Costa Rica and MMGY jumped on the digital nomad trend. The goal was to drive

awareness and deliver the new migratory visa for digital nomads. A message was communicated to the WeWork community of over 225,000 members across 132 U.S. and Canadian locations through a multifunctional approach that included digital screen takeovers, e-newsletters, and special surprise-and-delight, in-person events. Two of NYC's busiest locations were selected for takeovers, creating a *Pura Vida* experience amid a busy and industrial environment. The program resulted in nineteen digital nomads who traveled, providing an economic impact of $684,000 to Costa Rica for one year.

Julie's strategic partnerships for Costa Rica demonstrate the power of aligning with like-minded brands and leveraging complementary marketing channels to amplify impact, both social and economic. Successful brand partnerships involve a deep alignment of values, ensuring authenticity and effectiveness. Partnerships should also undergo a thorough vetting process to confirm the right brand fit, including considerations like shared audience demographics and complementary missions. While not all strategic partnerships focus on social impact, those that do tend to stand out, resonating deeply with audiences and building lasting trust and loyalty.

Challenges When Trying to Do Good

While the principles of conscious marketing are both admirable and increasingly essential in the landscape of business, implementing these strategies comes with challenges. Businesses striving to align their marketing efforts with ethical standards and social responsibility must navigate a cost implications, authenticity concerns, and balancing profit with purpose. Understanding these challenges and developing effective strategies to address them is crucial when developing your marketing mindset:

1. **Cost Implications:** One of the most significant challenges businesses face when adopting conscious marketing practices is the associated cost. Sustainable materials, ethical sourcing, and implementing comprehensive CSR initiatives often require substantial financial investment. For small to medium-sized enterprises (SMEs), these costs can be particularly burdensome and may strain limited budgets. The initial investment in sustainable technologies or processes may not yield immediate financial returns, making it difficult for businesses to justify.

   To mitigate cost concerns, businesses can adopt a phased approach to implementing conscious marketing initiatives. Prioritizing high-impact, cost-effective actions can create a foundation for more extensive efforts in the future. For example, a hotel might start by reducing single-use plastics before investing in renewable energy sources.

Additionally, leveraging partnerships and collaborations can help share costs and resources. Seeking grants, subsidies, or incentives for sustainable practices can also alleviate financial pressures.

2. **Authenticity Concerns:** In an era where consumers are highly attuned to brands' intentions, authenticity is paramount. Businesses risk greenwashing if their conscious marketing efforts are seen as superficial or insincere. Greenwashing not only damages a brand's reputation but also erodes consumer trust, which is difficult to rebuild once lost.

   Authenticity can be achieved by embedding conscious marketing into the company's mission and daily operations, rather than treating it as a mere marketing tactic. Walk the talk. Transparent communication about goals, processes, and progress is crucial. Companies should provide verifiable evidence of their commitments, such as third-party certifications, detailed sustainability reports, and case studies showcasing real impact. Engaging stakeholders, including employees, customers, and community members, in the development and implementation of CSR initiatives can also enhance authenticity and trust.

3. **Balancing Profit with Purpose:** Integrating conscious marketing requires balancing profitability with ethical goals to remain viable while making a positive impact. *To balance profit with purpose,*

businesses should identify areas where sustainability and profitability intersect. For instance, energy-efficient practices can reduce operational costs in the long run, and sustainable products can attract a loyal customer base willing to pay premium prices. Incorporating a value-driven approach where ethical practices enhance the brand's value proposition can also drive financial performance.

Setting clear, measurable goals that align with both profit and purpose can also help businesses track progress and demonstrate that ethical initiatives contribute to overall success. And viewing conscious marketing as an investment rather than an expense can guide companies to achieve a harmonious balance between profitability and social responsibility. As Niren Chaudhary, former chairman of Panera Brands, indicated to my students in our sustainability-focused marketing semester, "Doing the right thing is ultimately financially profitable."

4. **Internal Alignment and Employee Engagement:** Implementing conscious marketing requires buy-in from all levels of the organization. Misalignment between leadership and employees can hinder the effectiveness of CSR initiatives and dilute their impact. Employees need to understand and embrace the company's ethical commitments to ensure consistency and enthusiasm in executing conscious marketing strategies (internal marketing before external).

Fostering internal alignment begins with clear communication of the company's mission, values, and the importance of conscious marketing. Training and education on CSR initiatives empower employees to contribute meaningfully and feel invested in the company's goals. Creating opportunities for employee involvement in CSR projects, such as volunteer programs or sustainability committees, enhance engagement and ownership. And recognizing and rewarding employees who actively support and promote conscious marketing efforts can further reinforce the importance of these initiatives within the organizational culture.

5. **Measuring Impact and Demonstrating ROI:** Quantifying the impact of conscious marketing initiatives poses another significant challenge. Unlike traditional marketing metrics, the benefits of CSR activities, such as enhanced brand reputation, customer loyalty, and positive societal impact, are often intangible and difficult to measure. Without clear metrics, businesses may struggle to demonstrate the return on investment (ROI) of their ethical efforts, making it harder to justify continued or expanded commitments.

Evaluating Impact Success

To measure the success of conscious marketing, businesses should use tools like CSR impact assessments and sustainability reporting. These evaluations help quantify social and environmental contributions, ensuring marketing efforts align with broader ethical and sustainability goals.

Impact assessments analyze how a company's activities affect stakeholders—employees, customers, communities, and the environment. They reveal strengths and weaknesses in CSR initiatives, offering actionable insights to improve their overall impact.

Tracking key performance indicators (KPIs) tied to social and environmental goals—alongside financial metrics—helps businesses quantify their impact. Gathering qualitative feedback from customers, employees, and community members also offers insight into how CSR efforts are perceived.

By consistently measuring both tangible outcomes and intangible benefits, businesses can show the value of conscious marketing and build lasting stakeholder support. For instance, a hotel with a sustainability program might assess energy savings, improved waste management, and guest and staff satisfaction as part of its CSR impact evaluation.

Sustainability reporting refers to the regular disclosure of a company's environmental, social, and governance (ESG) performance. These reports communicate a company's commitment to sustainable practices and track progress toward long-term goals. Using recognized frameworks, like the Global Reporting Initiative (GRI) or the Sustainability Accounting Standards Board (SASB), adds credibility and consistency. In hospitality, such reports might include metrics on water use, carbon footprint, community engagement, and the promotion of local culture through partnerships and events.

Integrating CSR impact assessments and sustainability reporting into a conscious marketing strategy provides several key benefits. They:

1. Offer a clear mechanism for tracking progress, allowing businesses to celebrate successes and identify areas needing improvement.

2. Enhance accountability, ensuring that companies remain committed to their ethical promises and do not fall into the trap of greenwashing.

3. Foster trust and loyalty among consumers who increasingly prioritize sustainability and ethical practices in their purchasing decisions.

These evaluation tools support strategic decision-making by providing data-driven insights. For example, a hotel company might discover through its CSR impact assessment that its investment in renewable energy sources reduces operational costs in the long term and significantly boosts its brand image among environmentally conscious travelers. Additionally, sustainability reports can reveal trends and patterns that inform future marketing campaigns, ensuring they resonate with the target audience's values and expectations.

Incorporating CSR impact assessments and sustainability reporting also aligns with broader industry standards and consumer expectations. As regulatory bodies and industry organizations increasingly mandate openness and integrity in CSR activities, businesses that proactively adopt these practices position themselves as leaders in ethical marketing. This proactive stance not only mitigates risks associated with non-compliance but also differentiates brands and attracts customers who value integrity and responsible business practices.

Global Perspectives

CM in Retail and Other Service Sectors

To broaden our perspective on conscious marketing, let's explore inspiring examples from the retail and service sectors. These examples show that conscious marketing transcends industries and locations, with businesses naturally embracing hospitality by prioritizing people and community.

1. **Natura: Cultivating Sustainability in South America's Beauty Industry**

   Natura, a leading Brazilian cosmetics and personal care brand, undertakes initiatives such as:

- **Sustainable Sourcing:** Natura sources 100 percent of its ingredients from the Amazon rainforest, ensuring sustainable harvesting practices that benefit local communities and preserve biodiversity.
- **Eco-Friendly Packaging:** The company has significantly reduced its environmental footprint by developing biodegradable and recyclable packaging materials.
- **Social Programs:** Natura invests in social programs that support biodiversity conservation, women's empowerment, and community development in regions where they operate.

They assess their efforts and measure success with:

- **Environmental Impact Metrics:** Natura tracks reductions in carbon emissions, water usage, and waste through its sustainable sourcing and packaging initiatives.
- **Social Impact Assessments:** The company evaluates the effectiveness of its social programs by measuring improvements in local community livelihoods and biodiversity conservation outcomes.
- **Consumer Perception Surveys:** Regular surveys assess consumer awareness and perception of Natura's sustainability efforts,

showing increased trust and loyalty among customers.

- **Sales Growth:** There is a positive correlation between Natura's sustainability initiatives and sales growth, with the company experiencing a steady increase in revenue as consumers increasingly prefer eco-friendly and ethically produced products.

2. **Uniqlo: Pioneering Circular Fashion and Ethical Practices in Asia**

Uniqlo, a global apparel retailer based in Japan, has integrated conscious marketing into its business model through several key initiatives:

- **Recycling Programs:** Uniqlo has launched programs like "Re.Uniqlo," where customers can recycle their old Uniqlo clothing, which is then donated to those in need or repurposed into new products.

- **Sustainable Materials:** The brand focuses on using sustainable materials, such as recycled polyester, organic cotton, and down sourced from responsibly managed farms.

- **Energy Efficiency:** Uniqlo stores incorporate energy-efficient technologies, including LED lighting and solar panels, to reduce their environmental footprint.

They assess their efforts and measure success with:

- **Recycling Rates:** Uniqlo tracks the volume of clothing recycled through its initiatives, demonstrating tangible impacts on waste reduction.

- **Sustainability Reports:** The company publishes annual sustainability reports detailing progress on using sustainable materials and improving energy efficiency with key performance indicators (KPIs), such as the percentage of recycled materials used and reductions in energy consumption.

- **Brand Loyalty and Customer Engagement:** Uniqlo measures customer participation in recycling programs and monitors changes in brand loyalty through repeat purchases and customer feedback.

- **Market Expansion:** Success in sustainability has enabled Uniqlo to expand its market presence, particularly among environmentally conscious consumers, contributing to increased market share in key regions.

3. **IKEA: Leading the Charge Toward a Circular Economy in Europe**

IKEA, the Swedish multinational known for its affordable and stylish home furnishings, has embedded conscious marketing into its operations through extensive sustainability initiatives:

- **Circular Economy Commitment:** IKEA aims to become a circular business by 2030, focusing on designing products for reuse, repair, and recycling.

- **Renewable Energy Investments:** The company has invested heavily in renewable energy, installing solar panels on stores and investing in wind farms to power its operations.

- **Sustainable Product Lines:** IKEA offers a range of products made from sustainable materials, including FSC-certified wood and recycled plastics, and promotes energy-efficient appliances.

They assess their efforts and measure success with:

- **Environmental Performance Metrics:** IKEA monitors its renewable energy generation, carbon footprint, and waste reduction, reporting these metrics transparently in its sustainability reports.

- **Customer Adoption Rates:** The company tracks the sales and adoption rates of its sustainable product lines, analyzing consumer preferences and purchasing behaviors.

- **Supply Chain Audits:** Regular audits and assessments of their supply chain ensure compliance with sustainability standards, measuring improvements in sourcing practices and reducing environmental impact.

- **Corporate Partnerships and Certifications:** IKEA measures the success of its initiatives through partnerships with environmental organizations and achieving certifications, such as ISO 14001 for environmental management.

Conscious marketing can drive both positive social impact and business growth, serving as a model for other companies aspiring to adopt similar practices. I will continue to advocate for these initiatives in our hospitality marketing classes going forward.

Five Tips for Marketing CSR

1. **Define and Align CSR with Core Values**

   Successful CSR starts with clearly defining the company's core values and ensuring initiatives align with them, validating that CSR is an authentic extension of the brand rather than an add-on.

   Identify core values through stakeholder workshops, then select CSR projects that reflect them, such as environmental initiatives for sustainability-focused brands. Integrate these efforts into brand messaging, marketing, and storytelling to foster genuine internal and external engagement.

2. **Engage Stakeholders in the CSR Journey**

   CSR thrives when employees, customers, suppliers, and communities are actively involved. Their engagement ensures relevance, impact, and long-term success.

   Gather input through surveys, establish forums for feedback, and encourage partnerships with NGOs and businesses to amplify efforts. Regular updates on goals and progress build trust and transparency.

3. **Integrate CSR into the Marketing Strategy**

   CSR should be integrated into marketing efforts to enhance brand reputation and consumer trust, rather than standing alone.

   Showcase CSR efforts in campaigns, highlight impact through storytelling, and promote initiatives across social media, email, and the website. Align messaging with brand values to resonate with your audience.

4. **Communicate Transparently and Authentically**

   Trust in CSR comes from honest, data-backed communication. Openly sharing successes and challenges demonstrates accountability and commitment.

   Publish detailed reports, acknowledge setbacks, and use verified data to support claims. Avoid greenwashing. Credibility hinges on transparency and real results.

5. **Measure and Report Impact Effectively**
   Tracking CSR impact ensures effectiveness and continuous improvement. Clear reporting demonstrates value to stakeholders.

Use impact assessments and recognized reporting standards to track carbon reduction, volunteer hours, or community investment. Monitor progress and refine strategies. These steps will help get the process started and empower marketing professionals to lead the charge of conscious marketing. We want to ensure that their companies not only thrive economically but also uphold a commitment to making the world a better place.

Trends for Future CSR Marketing

The future of conscious marketing is driven by technological advancements, a growing demand for authentic brand activism, and an unwavering emphasis on ethical consumerism and conscious purchasing. By embracing advanced personalization through AI and big data marketers can drive significant positive change.

With knowledge of these influences, marketing professionals can anticipate and respond to the evolving expectations of consumers, positioning businesses as leaders in the movement toward a better world.

Marketing Mantras

Businesses can create meaningful connections with consumers and drive positive societal and environmental impact. Conscious marketing transcends traditional profit-driven strategies to foster trust and loyalty.

Additionally, we highlighted here the significance of forming purposeful partnerships that align with shared values, amplifying both brand visibility and community impact. Real-world examples, including MMGY Global's successful collaborations for Costa Rica's tourism and impactful student-led projects, illustrate how integrating ethical practices and collaborative efforts can lead to sustainable growth and enduring relationships. *This shows us the essential shift from merely "selling products" to "building brands that genuinely contribute to the greater good."*

1. **Shift from Profit-Driven to Purpose-Driven:** Conscious marketing is not about tacking on a CSR initiative for appearances; it's about operating from a values-based approach.

2. **Empower Consumers Through Authenticity:** Modern audiences, especially younger consumers, research brands before making decisions. Genuine proof of ethical initiatives—like meaningful local partnerships or transparent business practices—builds trust and loyalty far beyond generic claims.

3. **Expand Reach and Multiply Good Through Partnerships:** Collaborations that unite businesses and community stakeholders around shared goals create a ripple effect. By pooling resources, expertise, and networks, partners can amplify positive impact while strengthening brand awareness and stakeholder relationships.

4. **Elevate Brand Identity with Local Engagement:** Whether it's beach cleanups, clothing drives for local charities, or art-focused community events, hyper-local initiatives demonstrate a brand's commitment to making a direct, tangible difference.

5. **Fuel Long-Term Viability with Conscious Marketing:** Aligning brand strategy with ethical values, stakeholder needs, and transparent storytelling drives sustainable growth. This holistic approach resonates across demographics, positioning brands to thrive in a market that increasingly rewards authenticity and purposeful actions.

# # #

By examining strategic partnerships and their challenges, we emphasized how conscious marketing benefits both businesses and society at large. As we transition to the next chapter, we focus on reviewing our end goals, highlighting the significance of measuring our marketing efforts against the key performance indicators (KPIs) we established at the outset. This analysis will enable us to evaluate our success and accountability in achieving our marketing objectives, ensuring our strategies align with our overarching vision.

Marketing Mindset in Motion

Marketing isn't just about selling. It's about making a meaningful impact. Think of a brand that has successfully aligned its marketing with a greater purpose, whether through sustainability, social responsibility, or community engagement. What made their approach authentic and effective? Now, consider your brand or business. How can you integrate conscious marketing into your strategy in a way that builds trust and delivers real impact, authentically?

8

Review the End Goals

Whenever we start any marketing journey, it's crucial to begin with a clear understanding of our goals. In *Developing Your Marketing Mindset: Real-World Lessons from Hospitality*, we dedicated a whole chapter to setting measurable objectives because they're the foundation for every strategy and decision. *Start with the end goals.* These goals act as a roadmap, guiding us in a way that aligns perfectly with our brand's bigger vision. But just setting those goals isn't enough. We also need to check in regularly and see how our marketing efforts are stacking up. By connecting with customers through the techniques we've discussed, we can determine if our approach is effective, and make any necessary adjustments to enhance our impact.

This is where data and measurement come into play. How do we know if our marketing efforts hit the mark? Did we pick the right KPIs to track? Did our campaigns get the likes, shares, bookings, or sales we hoped for? Or even better, surpass those expectations? Did testing show us that one message worked better for a certain audience than another? These are the questions we'll explore as we dive into gauging success and fine-tuning our marketing tactics.

To make sense of all this, it helps to understand two key types of measurement: *quantitative* and *qualitative*. Quantitative data is all about the numbers, such as website visits, sales, and conversion rates that we can count and analyze. It gives us a clear snapshot of performance and trends. But the story doesn't end there. Qualitative data digs a little deeper, capturing how customers feel and what they think. This could be feedback from surveys, social media comments, or even the tone of conversations around our brand. Quantitative data tells us *what* happened; qualitative data helps explain *why* it happened. Together, they give us the full picture needed to sharpen our strategies and hit our marketing goals.

Data Analysis and Measurement

Systematically reviewing our goals provides valuable insights into what worked and what didn't. This evaluation highlights successes and uncovers opportunities, enabling us to make informed decisions for future campaigns. By periodically reviewing key performance indicators (KPIs) -- sales, conversions, engagement metrics, and creative elements -- we can gain valuable insights.

Ultimately, reviewing the end goals is about fostering a culture of accountability and continuous learning within the marketing strategy. Regularly assessing performance against initial objectives ensures that marketing initiatives remain aligned with business goals, driving sustained growth and success.

Intangible, Holistic Return on Investment (ROI)

"If it doesn't lead to conversation, then don't waste the marketing dollars. This is why digital marketing is so powerful, because in real time, we can measure its effectiveness. But in class, we also did learn about the intangible ROI, and that's a harder 'sell' to an owner. We know as marketers that it's critical to respect the intangible; our job is to prove it while also showing effective revenues. "The famous retailer John Wanamaker is thought to have said, 'Half the money I spend on advertising is wasted; the trouble is I don't know which half.' In a world with an abundance of data where everyone is trying to measure returns, I think it's important to recognize that some marketing initiatives will not have a direct way to measure return. If a restaurant offers a free dessert for someone's birthday, or a hotel places a complimentary bottle of champagne in a room for a couple's anniversary, there

may not be any immediate financial return, however, there is an intangible return to building a relationship with a consumer. They are likely to remember these acts and visit the hotel or restaurant again. Repeat business is key for the hospitality industry, and a free dessert or bottle of champagne is an important investment, even if you can't immediately measure the ROI." Marut K. Raval, BU School of Hospitality, Class of 2020, MMH 2021

What kind of value-add, remarkable moment, or innovative experience can you offer your clients/guests to help build memories, foster loyalty, and create lifetime customers? That return on investment is invaluable.

Marketing Accountability and Comprehensive Approaches

Traditionally, marketing accountability has focused on setting objectives and assessing performance metrics. However, there is an opportunity to adopt a more comprehensive approach. This involves collecting data while also deriving meaningful insights. It requires understanding the factors that influence customer perceptions and drive their behaviors. Additionally, it means taking responsibility for building relationships with key stakeholders by addressing their needs, desires, and interests, all while maintaining authenticity both within the organization and in external interactions.

Branding and marketing efforts must consistently demonstrate accountability, ensuring that financial investments generate the intended impact and contribute to the company's overall profitability. Often, return on investment is evaluated solely using quantitative metrics, such as the number of social shares, clicks, sales. However, incorporating qualitative measures can provide valuable context to these numerical data points.

In hospitality, while metrics like conversion and occupancy rates are important, understanding the key factors that influence customer behavior and drive their actions is equally crucial. Engaging in conversations with customers to learn why they value the brand and understanding why some customers choose competitors, while ensuring that internal stakeholders are aware of the brand's values and customer expectations -- are essential for gaining deeper, insightful information.

While not all marketing investments yield immediate revenue, many are designed to build long-term brand loyalty and awareness. These initiatives—though slower to show returns—contribute meaningfully to the bottom line over time through consistent execution and reinforcement. Balancing both qualitative and quantitative assessments offers a fuller picture of marketing effectiveness.

ROI can also be assessed purely based on marketing expenditures. The most widely used method for calculating return on marketing investment (ROMI) involves subtracting the costs of goods sold and marketing expenses from the revenue generated by marketing, then dividing that figure by the marketing spend. While these quantitative measures can help demonstrate progress toward marketing goals, adopting a holistic approach to ROI evaluation is essential for a more complete and accurate assessment.

> *"KPIs are a great way to create a benchmark for success, but oftentimes, the intangible ROI is even more important, especially in the hospitality industry. Our industry is essentially in the business of creating experiences and memories. How can someone measure people's experiences or memories? It is quite a difficult feat.*

> *"Rather than fixating solely on the revenue, views, shares, impressions, etc., businesses can benefit from focusing on creating the best possible experience for all guests, not just VIPs, to ensure positive memories are created. Once a positive memory is established, that person is likely to tell others about their experience. Word of mouth (WOM) may be hard to measure, but it can often make or break a business. As we continue into the digital age, this is something companies should continue to keep in mind and prioritize."* Jamie Weber, BU School of Hospitality, Class of 2020

Metric Type	Description
Quantitative Metrics	Quantitative metrics focus on numbers—measurable data that show how marketing efforts perform. Examples include website visits, conversion rates, sales figures, click-through rates, and social media follower counts. These metrics provide clear benchmarks, help track trends over time, and enable data-driven decisions.
Qualitative Metrics	Qualitative metrics capture the feelings, opinions, and experiences behind the numbers. They come from customer feedback, online reviews, social media comments, and focus groups. These insights explain *why* customers behave a certain way and reveal motivations and preferences that numbers alone can't.

Data Driven ROI

Pete Rosenblum's firm, Map360, works with entertainment venues, comedy shops, arenas, and stadiums, and specializes in experiential events and working with influencers. Pete explains the need for data to help make decisions and prove that marketing is worthy to the large-scale, big block buster clients:

> "We use data to take a deep dive into audiences, reach, potential impressions, cost, and proper targeting for any digital campaign we are getting ready to launch. That's super-important to

understand the different options and to suggest the best paths for a client or project.

"For an experiential or influencer campaign, we operate a little bit in reverse—maybe looking at potential reach or impressions, but then gathering all the data we get *after* the campaign. We put together what we call ROX reports, return on experience. A ROX is a deep dive into numbers and data after an experience."

This same data-driven mindset is carried into the classroom, where students apply analytical tools and strategic thinking to real-world hospitality challenges.

Student: Vivian Feinstein-Gough

School: BU School of Hospitality, Master of Management in Hospitality

Graduation: Class of 2020

The Marketing Challenge: The class of master's students assessed the online presence for the Lyons Group restaurant, Game On, located on Lansdowne Street in Boston, at Fenway Park. The students reviewed the online visibility of the restaurant's competitive set, conducted a review of the efficacy of the front end and back end of the website, looked at potential SEO opportunities, assessed the online reputation through review sites, and suggested tweaks to social media outreach and marketing of events.

Outcome: The restaurant group's director of marketing and social media manager attended the final presentation. Recommendations were well received and acknowledged. The venue offers a fun and interactive experience, and the goal was to enhance this and replicate it online as an interactive game to better represent the brand.

Vivian's Insight: "In navigating the complex landscape of digital marketing, KPIs and ROI have become pivotal metrics guiding our strategies. From our class project examining Search Engine Marketing (paid search) and Google Ads effectiveness, I learned the importance of measurable outcomes. However, KPIs run deeper than 'how many interactions did this campaign get' or 'what was the cost per click.'

"In my role with the hotel group in Belize, I needed to attribute revenue to our marketing campaigns. After the digital marketing course, I realized that our resorts lacked an online booking platform, making it difficult to directly attribute revenue to our digital campaigns. This gap highlighted the need for infrastructure improvements to accurately gauge marketing effectiveness.

"Implementing a booking platform not only allowed for precise ROI calculations but also emphasized the necessity of associating marketing expenditures with tangible revenue generation. My approach to ROI differs from traditional models. Beyond campaign-specific metrics, I factor in all associated costs, from outsourced agency fees to the condo owner payout. This holistic view ensures that each marketing initiative not only drives top-line growth but also contributes meaningfully to our bottom-line profitability, a vital consideration for both marketing effectiveness and business sustainability."

Both Pete and Vivian comment on the pivotal role of data-driven accountability in achieving meaningful return on investment (ROI) in marketing. Pete claims the necessity of leveraging comprehensive data analysis to demonstrate the value of marketing initiatives to large-scale clients. By utilizing metrics, such as audience reach, potential impressions, and post-campaign ROX (return on experience) reports, he ensures that every campaign is targeted effectively and measures the experiential impact.

Vivian insightfully discusses the holistic approach, which considers all associated costs and emphasizes tangible revenue generation. Together, these cases tell us that marketing accountability depends on the capacity to measure and analyze relevant data meticulously. With data-driven strategies, marketers can validate efforts and continuously refine approaches.

Key Marketing Metrics

Accurately measuring and analyzing the impact of your efforts is essential. To streamline this process, focus on a curated set of key marketing metrics to provide a clear structure for evaluating the effectiveness of the strategies and identifying areas that may require modification:

1. Customer acquisition cost (CAC) is a fundamental metric that encompasses the total expenses associated with acquiring a new customer, including both marketing and sales costs. By evaluating CAC, businesses can assess the efficiency of their spending and ensure that the resources allocated to customer acquisition are yielding desirable results. This metric is closely related to both marketing cost metrics and the lifetime value vs. CAC ratio, providing a comprehensive view of acquisition efficiency.

2. Customer lifetime value (CLV) predicts the total revenue a customer is expected to generate throughout their relationship with your company. Assessing CLV allows businesses to understand the long-term value of their customer base compared to acquisition costs, ensuring sustainable growth. This metric integrates insights from lifetime value vs. CAC and customer retention metrics, highlighting the importance of maintaining a loyal customer base alongside acquiring new customers.

3. The conversion rate measures the percentage of leads or website visitors who complete a desired action, such as making a purchase, signing up for a newsletter, booking a hotel room, or making a restaurant reservation. This metric is crucial

for determining the effectiveness of marketing efforts in driving tangible outcomes. The conversion rate provides a measure of campaign success in turning prospects into customers.

4. Return on marketing investment (ROMI) calculates the revenue generated for every dollar spent on marketing, offering an indicator of the profitability and efficiency of marketing campaigns. ROMI draws from marketing cost metrics and key performance indicators (KPIs), ensuring that marketing investments are aligned with financial returns and overall business objectives.

   These metrics have evolved in some cases: My friend JoAnne Borselli at Connelly Partners explains that the media department in her agency uses "cost-per-x" as an optimization tool. For example, if we strive for less investment for more results, and the cost-per-conversion is tracked over time, we can determine if we've achieved more action for less money, over time. This is a more straightforward approach for measuring the decrease in spend and increase in bookings or conversations.

5. Website traffic and engagement encompass the total number of visitors to your website, along with their interactions, such as page views and time spent on the site. This metric serves as a barometer for the reach and engagement level of online presence. By integrating website and SEO metrics, audience engagement metrics,

and bounce rate, it provides a holistic view of how effectively your website attracts and retains visitors. (Bounce rate measures the percentage of visitors who navigate away from your site after viewing only a single page, without engaging further or visiting any other pages within the same session. In other words, it indicates how many users "bounce" away from your website after landing on just one page.)

6. Social media engagement evaluates interactions on social platforms, including likes, shares, comments, and follower growth. This metric gauges a brand's presence and audience interaction across social channels.

7. Email marketing performance tracks metrics such as open rates, click-through rates (CTR), and conversion rates from email campaigns. This metric is vital for evaluating how well email marketing efforts engage and convert subscribers. By incorporating aspects of A/B testing and experimentation, it ensures that email strategies are both personalized and optimized for maximum impact.

8. Customer satisfaction and feedback include metrics like Net Promoter Score (NPS), customer satisfaction (CSAT) scores, and online reviews. These indicators offer valuable insights into customer experiences and perceptions of your brand, integrating feedback from guest satisfaction surveys and other sources to identify areas

for improvement to enhance overall customer relations.

9. Channel attribution assigns credit to different marketing channels and touchpoints that contribute to conversions. This metric is essential for understanding the effectiveness of each marketing channel, allowing for optimized resource allocation.

10. Sales growth measures the increase in sales revenue over a specific period, reflecting the overall impact of conversion and customer retention metrics, providing a clear indicator of how marketing efforts translate into tangible business outcomes.

As we conclude our focus on reviewing the end goals and meaningful metrics, it's important to consider *how* those goals will be measured. A thoughtful measurement plan bridges the gap between aspirations and outcomes, aligning goals with the specific methods we will use to track progress and adjust strategies as needed. (All this is referenced in *Developing Your Marketing Mindset: Real-World Lessons from Hospitality* in the chapter "Start with the End Goals.")

Rather than waiting to assess success with a wrap-up report, this approach emphasizes continuous monitoring and learning along the way. Now, let's review the key takeaways that will help us create goals that are strategic, measurable, and manageable throughout this process.

Marketing Mantras

1. **Establish Clear and Measurable End Goals:** Define specific, measurable end goals before launching any marketing campaign. For example, a luxury hotel aiming to increase direct bookings by 20 percent within six months can focus on enhancing website functionality and launching targeted email campaigns. Clear objectives allow for progress tracking through relevant KPIs, ensuring marketing efforts align with desired outcomes.

2. **Embrace a Holistic ROI Approach:** Move beyond traditional ROI calculations that focus solely on immediate financial returns. Identify both quantitative metrics, like sales growth, and qualitative metrics, such as customer satisfaction, relevant to your campaigns. This balanced approach reveals marketing effectiveness and fosters long-term relationships, generating immediate revenue while building enduring brand equity.

3. **Integrate Quantitative and Qualitative Metrics:** Combine quantitative metrics, such as clicks and social shares, with qualitative assessments, like customer feedback and focus groups. For instance, an online retailer can track clicks and shares while conducting customer interviews to understand the motivations behind these actions.

This view enables us to refine strategies based on actual customer preferences and emerging trends.

4. **Foster a Culture of Accountability and Continuous Learning:** Regularly review marketing performance against initial objectives to encourage accountability and improvement. For instance, a regional spa chain aiming to boost online bookings by 15 percent can analyze monthly results to identify successful strategies. Discussions about successes and setbacks promote a learning environment, allowing teams to refine tactics and adapt to market changes.

5. **Leverage Data for Informed Decision-Making:** Continually analyze KPIs to gain insights into audience behavior and strategy performance. For example, a luxury hotel can track metrics like engagement rates and booking conversions to determine the most effective marketing channels. This data-driven approach enables resource allocation toward high-performing strategies while optimizing or discontinuing less-effective ones.

# # #

As we conclude this chapter, remember, measuring our marketing efforts is not a one-time task but an ongoing commitment. By consistently evaluating our progress and comparing it with our KPIs, we can ensure that our strategies are effective and aligned with our brand's objectives. As we transition to the next chapter, which concludes our section on "Connecting with Your Audience"—the very essence of marketing—we will explore how the principles of hospitality can elevate our marketing efforts, creating a valuable differentiation and distinct competitive edge that resonates with customers on a personal level.

Marketing Mindset in Motion

Understanding your return on investment is crucial for sustainable success. Reflect on the metrics you've been tracking. Are they aligned with your overarching business goals? How can you incorporate both tangible and intangible ROI into your analysis? Consider the broader impact of your marketing efforts, including brand perception and customer loyalty. As you evaluate your strategies, ask yourself: What adjustments can you make to enhance your accountability and effectiveness? How will you ensure that your marketing decisions are driven by data, leading to improved outcomes?

9

Harness the Hospitality

Hospitality has shaped my career and fueled my passion for decades. It's a force that naturally connects those of us who care deeply about making people feel welcome, seen, and valued. My years as a professional in the industry—as a consultant, marketer, consumer, and traveler—have led me to a simple but powerful realization: Every business can and *should* harness the hospitality. Any service-driven organization must embrace the art of making others feel heard and cared for. And the way we communicate, position, and market our businesses—whatever the product or service—should reflect the same compassion, empathy, and genuine warmth that make hospitality so enduringly successful.

I hope by now you understand that hospitality is more than just an industry. It embodies a mindset that can transform marketing strategies across various sectors. The principles of hospitality—anticipation, personalization, exceptional service, innovative and memorable experiences—are not exclusive to hotels and restaurants; they are vital components for any business aiming to connect with its audience. By adopting an approach driven by generosity and warmth, marketers can foster deeper relationships and create meaningful interactions that resonate with customers.

As shared in *Developing Your Marketing Mindset: Real-World Lessons from Hospitality*, I reference several philosophies of hospitality, including *enlightened hospitality* and *unreasonable hospitality*. Enlightened hospitality, coined and championed by New York restaurateur Danny Meyer, emphasizes the idea (among many mantras in his toolkit) that taking exceptional care of employees ultimately leads to better customer experiences and, in turn, business success. Will Guidara's unreasonable hospitality builds on this by encouraging businesses to deliver beyond what's expected—creating moments of surprise and delight that make guests feel genuinely special. Both philosophies underscore a deeper truth: Hospitality is not just about service; it's about how you make people feel.

Another concept that aligns with these philosophies, though it may initially seem off-putting to some, is *servant leadership*. This term, which has been used for decades, describes a leadership approach that prioritizes the needs of others—employees, customers, and the broader community—above the leader's own ambitions. Phrased by

Robert K. Greenleaf in his 1970 essay "The Servant as Leader," the philosophy challenges the traditional top-down leadership model by focusing on empowerment, empathy, and stewardship. Servant leadership does not imply weakness; rather, it signifies a commitment to guiding and supporting others to help them reach their full potential. In the hospitality industry, this mindset is crucial; those of us in the business succeed when we genuinely care about the people we serve, whether they are our guests or our teams. By embracing these principles, we create meaningful, lasting experiences that set exceptional hospitality apart.

Effective marketing extends beyond merely responding to customer needs. It involves proactively crafting experiences that evoke loyalty and forge emotional connections. Great hospitality is about understanding the audience's desires and expectations, allowing us to design marketing initiatives that meet those needs and exceed them. This proactive approach sets the foundation for remarkable moments that keep guests or customers coming back.

Marketers should aspire to think like hoteliers, restaurateurs or guest experience specialists, focusing on strategies that make customers feel seen, valued, and understood.

By embodying the essence of hospitality in marketing efforts, we create an environment where customers feel welcomed and appreciated. This chapter serves as a bridge between the marketing techniques we've explored throughout the book and the hospitality mindset that elevates those techniques, showcasing how these principles can create a distinct competitive edge.

As we bring together the core lessons of this book, please appreciate how adopting a hospitality-driven mindset enhances customer experiences and drives impactful marketing results. Whether we operate in the hospitality sector or any other industry, the ability to anticipate and respond to customer needs with genuine care is paramount.

In harnessing the principles of hospitality, businesses can set themselves apart in a crowded marketplace, transforming transactional interactions into lasting relationships. Let's see how the integration of these hospitality principles into our marketing strategies can elevate our brand and create a lasting impact on our audience.

Essentials of Hospitality-Driven Marketing

To effectively connect with customers and create lasting relationships, we must embrace the core principles of hospitality-driven marketing. These, what I term "essentials"—anticipation, personalization, attention to detail, and seamless consistency—serve as guiding frameworks that can transform any business. By drawing from best practices in the hospitality industry, we can elevate our marketing strategies, ensuring they resonate deeply with our audiences and foster emotional connections that drive loyalty and engagement.

1. **Anticipation: Marketing That Knows What Customers Want, Before They Do**

   In the hospitality industry, luxury hotels in particular, exemplify the power of anticipation through pre-stay personalization. By utilizing customer relationship management (CRM) systems, hotels gather detailed guest preferences, allowing them to tailor experiences even before the guest arrives. For example, a hotel might know a returning guest prefers a specific type of pillow or enjoys certain amenities, ensuring their stay feels uniquely crafted for them. In broader marketing, businesses can apply this principle by leveraging data analytics, customer behavior insights, and social listening tools to predict customer needs and desires. By anticipating these wants, brands can deliver relevant content and offers to enhance customer satisfaction and loyalty.

2. **Personalization: The Difference Between a "Guest" and a "Customer"**

   High-end restaurants excel in creating memorable experiences through personalized service, often with staff who remember frequent customers' preferences. This attention to detail transforms a dining experience from mere "service" to a "relationship." Applying this to marketing, brands can enhance engagement and loyalty by delivering customized content and targeted messaging. By utilizing customer data, businesses can craft hyper-personalized experiences, such as specific email campaigns or product recommendations based on past purchases. This approach makes guests feel appreciated and understood, strengthening their connection to the brand.

3. **The Power of Small Details: Surprise and Delight in Marketing**

The philosophy of surprise and delight is deeply rooted in the principles of hospitality. These concepts emphasize putting the guest first and creating emotional connections through unexpected gestures. In marketing, small, thoughtful details—such as handwritten notes or personalized follow-ups—can elevate customer experiences to new emotional heights.

Similarly, in marketing, brands can incorporate surprise elements that elevate the consumer experience. For instance, a handwritten follow-up after a purchase or a special rate for a customer's birthday can leave a lasting impact. These unexpected gestures demonstrate that a brand values its customers, reinforcing emotional ties and encouraging repeat business.

During a recent stay at the M Gallery Hotel (Accor) in Strasbourg, France, this philosophy came to life for me in a memorable way. The front desk team had noted it was my wedding anniversary and thoughtfully curated daily sightseeing recommendations for my husband and me. Each evening, we returned to our room to find a delightful surprise—whether it was two small bottles of champagne, balloons with chocolates, or handwritten notes from the concierge asking about our day and suggesting tours for the next. These unexpected touches brought genuine smiles and made us feel truly valued, reminding me how small acts of kindness can create lasting emotional connections between brands and their guests.

4. **Seamlessness and Consistency: The Omnichannel Hospitality Approach**

   The Ritz-Carlton is renowned for its legendary service consistency, where every guest interaction reflects the brand's values, regardless of the channel. This seamless experience is crucial in hospitality and is equally vital in marketing. Ensuring that physical, digital, and human touchpoints are aligned allows customers to engage with a brand effortlessly. For instance, a customer should receive consistent messaging across social media, email campaigns, and in-store experiences. By creating a frictionless, memorable brand experience, businesses strengthen customer connection and reinforce their brand identity.

Marketing Hospitality Beyond Hospitality

Today, the principles of hospitality extend far beyond the limits of the hotel and restaurant sector; businesses in various industries are recognizing the value of hospitality-inspired marketing, using it to create memorable customer experiences that foster loyalty and engagement. By adopting a hospitality-driven mindset, companies can transform how they interact with customers, ensuring that every touchpoint reflects care, attention, and personalization. Let's take a quick look at two very influential business brands and sectors, Apple and luxury retail, and identify how they implement these principles to enhance customer relationships and elevate marketing strategies.

Apple's Retail Experience:

Apple stores exemplify a hospitality-driven approach by treating customers like hotel guests rather than mere shoppers. Employees, known as "geniuses," are trained to engage with customers on a personal level, offering individualized support and creating an inviting atmosphere, enhancing the overall shopping experience.

Apple also utilizes customer feedback to refine service offerings continuously. The Genius Bar appointments are designed to minimize wait times and maximize customer interaction, mirroring the bespoke service found in luxury hotels. By creating an environment where customers can receive help with their devices while enjoying a coffee or browsing products in a relaxed setting, Apple cultivates an immersive and welcoming experience that keeps customers coming back.

Luxury Retail and White-Glove Service:

Luxury retailers, such as Neiman Marcus and Saks Fifth Avenue, have long embraced hospitality-inspired marketing through "white-glove service." They offer personalized shopping appointments and curated experiences, where stylists provide one-on-one consultations for individual preferences. Loyalty programs further enhance this approach by rewarding repeat customers with exclusive benefits, creating an elevated shopping experience.

These retailers also focus on creating an environment that feels exclusive and inviting. From lavish store designs to complimentary refreshments, every detail is curated to create exceptional moments for customers, fostering emotional connections that extend beyond the transaction. Investing in the customer experience allows luxury retailers to cultivate brand loyalty and repeat business.

Utilizing principles of hospitality, these companies remind us that exceptional customer service can transcend traditional boundaries, providing valuable lessons for any industry.

Infuse Hospitality into Marketing

To leverage the power of hospitality in marketing, let's audit current strategies through a hospitality lens. Begin by asking fundamental questions: Do our customers feel welcomed and valued? Assess our communication and engagement tactics; are we merely responding to their inquiries, or are we proactively anticipating their needs?

Next, examine the seamlessness of the experience we provide throughout the customer journey. In hospitality, consistency is paramount; guests should feel the same level of service whether they interact with our website, social media, or customer support. Ensure that messaging is coherent and reflects our brand's values, every time. Disjointed experiences lead to frustration and disengagement, while a seamless journey enhances customer satisfaction and retention.

Infusing hospitality into our marketing strategy also requires adopting a "host" mentality. As marketers, we should strive to exemplify gracious hosts, ensuring every interaction with customers is intentional, warm, and engaging. This mindset encourages marketers to consider the audience's feelings and experiences, creating an environment where customers feel cared for and appreciated. When customers feel like guests in your brand's space, they are more likely to develop emotional connections and loyalty.

How do we do this? One practical way to implement this host mentality is through personalized communication. Take the time to craft messages to individual customers, using data insights to address their specific needs and preferences. Utilize CRM systems to track customer interactions and preferences, ensuring that communication and marketing efforts reflect a genuine understanding of your audience.

Create opportunities for engagement that go beyond transactions. Encourage customer feedback, host events, or create content that invites participation. This not only helps customers feel involved but also builds a community around the brand.

The Virgin brand is all about delivering bold, memorable experiences that blend fun, comfort, and a touch of unexpected delight—whether you're flying Virgin Airlines, staying at Virgin Hotels, or cruising with Virgin Voyages. What sets Virgin apart is how it consistently carries its vibrant personality and customer-first values across every offering.

For example, on a Virgin Airlines flight, I was surprised and delighted when flight attendants gave passenger cozy burgundy cotton pajamas. I actually wore them and slept comfortably on the plane. The playfully named sundry bag, packed with essentials like toothpaste, an eye mask, and other beauty goodies, added to the experience. Each touchpoint is playful yet polished, fun yet practical. Each interaction reflects Virgin's signature knack for surprising and delighting customers—a fundamental element of their marketing strategy and brand promise.

What is Experiential Marketing?

Experiential marketing focuses on creating meaningful, memorable interactions between a brand and its customers by engaging their senses, emotions, and experiences. Rather than simply promoting a product or service, it seeks to immerse people in a brand's story through events, environments, or moments to evoke feelings and forge lasting connections.

My recent stay at the Graduate Hotel in Nashville beautifully exemplifies experiential marketing in action. Amid the profound grief I felt after losing my brother, the hotel's distinctive design, warm atmosphere, and playful sensory details became far more than just aesthetic touches; they offered genuine emotional comfort and uplifted me during an incredibly difficult time. This ability to create an environment that resonated so personally highlights how thoughtful experience design serves as a powerful marketing tool. With design elements that evoked smiles, moments of joy, and an environment of comfort, the Graduate Nashville didn't simply provide a place to stay; it delivered a memorable experience that allowed me to smile even in moments of pain. It also inspired a desire to return under happier circumstances. Marketing and experience are intertwined, and each aims to create lasting moments that stay with guests long after their visit.

Interestingly, just days after my return from this Nashville hotel, eHotelier published a brief article about "experiential dining" (eHotelier, 2025). It reveals that experiential dining has "evolved far beyond themed décor or theatrical chef's tables; today, it focuses on creating an emotional journey for guests, transforming a meal into a meaningful memory through storytelling, sensory design, and personalized touches." Guests now expect dining to deliver excellent food *and* a shareable story that connects them to a sense of place and purpose.

To achieve this, hotels and restaurants are layering subtle sensory elements, sound, scent, lighting, and texture, alongside thoughtful service and local collaborations. Personalized service, interactive dishes, and connections with local communities and artisans deepen the authenticity of the experience, and avoid stale traditions.

Successful experiential dining is about creating intimacy and soul, not just spectacle. It depends on energized, supported teams who feel ownership and pride in their service. Today's guests also expect sustainability, inclusivity, and menu transparency as fundamental. Ultimately, the heart of experiential dining and marketing is about making people feel something memorable and real, using every element of the environment and the story to forge a genuine connection.

The Future of Hospitality-Driven Marketing

I can't stress this enough. *Hospitality is a meaningful differentiator in business and in marketing.* Companies that prioritize a hospitality-driven approach create memorable experiences that resonate with customers, setting themselves apart from competitors.

As we consider the implications of hospitality in marketing, a guiding mantra arises: "Make them feel 'good' wherever they are." This philosophy encourages marketers to prioritize warmth, personalization, and attentiveness in every interaction. When customer experiences have become a competitive space, it reminds us that *the human element remains at the heart of successful marketing*.

This forward-thinking approach elevates our critical and strategic mindsets and fosters a culture of continuous improvement. As marketers, we must take actionable steps to apply specific communication techniques that promote problem-solving and customer solutions. As Maya Angelou famously said, "People will forget what you said, people will forget what you did, but people will never forget how you made them feel." This wisdom serves as a reminder that engaging with our audience meaningfully (applying the communication and marketing techniques shared in these pages, for example) leads to higher satisfaction and loyalty.

Hospitality is about how you make people feel.

Embracing hospitality in marketing is a transformative mindset that has the potential to redefine customer relationships. By making customers feel "at home," "comfortable," and "good," and by analyzing our strategies through a hospitality lens, we can bring our marketing efforts to new heights through thoughtful engagement.

As we conclude this journey through my simplified interpretations of marketing principles, which I've enjoyed teaching to university students, it's essential to recognize that the principles we've explored extend far beyond traditional business frameworks. *Marketing Mindset in Motion: Inspired by Hospitality* serves as a reminder that marketing is a dynamic, evolving practice that thrives on understanding and anticipating the needs of others. The concepts discussed in each chapter, from foundational marketing strategies to the nuanced understanding of customer connection, empower us as marketers and leaders.

This book has also emphasized that *hospitality is not merely an industry.*

Hospitality is a mindset that serves as a powerful competitive advantage.

Thank you for journeying with me through these pages. I hope you have noted your own mantras from these examples and insights. Everyone can benefit from a marketing mindset, and all of us have something to learn from the generous, people-centered world of hospitality and tourism.

Marketing Mantras

1. **Anticipate Needs, Exceed Expectations. Provide Suprise and Delight** to further elevate the experience in surprising ways. Embrace a proactive approach to understanding what your customers want before they even ask.

2. **Personalization is Power.** Create individualized experiences that make customers feel valued and understood, transforming them from mere transactions into loyal advocates.

3. **The Little Things Matter.** Recognize that small gestures, thoughtful details, and delightful moments can create emotional connections that elevate the customer experience.

4. **Seamless Experiences Build Trust.** Ensure consistency across all touchpoints, providing a frictionless journey that allows customers to feel at home wherever they interact with your brand. Prioritize emotional connections and make them feel "good" wherever they are connecting with you.

5. **Be the Gracious Host.** Adopt a host mentality in every marketing interaction, ensuring that each customer feels welcomed, engaged, and appreciated.

6. **Differentiate Through Hospitality.** Use hospitality-inspired marketing as a secret weapon to distinguish your brand, foster loyalty and gain a competitive advantage.

Marketing Mindset in Motion

As we consider the principles of hospitality-driven marketing, take a moment to ask yourself: Are you actively anticipating your customers' needs and desires? How do you ensure that your messaging feels personalized and thoughtful? Reflect on the small details in your marketing efforts; what gestures or surprises can you incorporate to delight your customers? Are you maintaining consistency across all touchpoints to create seamless experiences? How can you embody the "gracious host" mentality in every interaction, making customers feel truly valued and "at home" or "good"? By thoughtfully answering these questions, you can elevate your marketing strategy and foster deeper connections with your audience.

Mindset in Motion Scorecard

Let's revisit our scorecard to assess any shifts in our marketing mindset in action. Remember, as we move forward, it is essential to embrace the hospitality sensibilities woven throughout this book and watch as it transforms marketing strategies into meaningful connections that inspire loyalty and drive success.

From identifying and understanding our audience to strengthening digital and physical presence, delivering compelling presentations, embracing conscious marketing, and measuring results, each chapter has reinforced the importance of an intentional and adaptable marketing approach. Let's use this scorecard to help us review the last few chapters; let's determine if we are already thinking about fine-tuning our strategies, sharpening our messages, and ensuring our marketing efforts are both customer-centric and results-driven.

How to Use This Scorecard:

- **Self-Assess:** At the end of each section, rate yourself on a scale from 1 to 5 in the designated categories.
- **Reflect:** Consider the guiding questions to evaluate your application of key concepts.
- **Refine:** Identify areas for growth and revisit earlier chapters to strengthen your marketing mindset.

Connecting with Your (Guests or) Customers

(Reviewing content from Chapters 4–9)

Milestone: From Passive Engagement to Meaningful Connection

Concept	1 (Needs Work)	3 (Getting There)	5 (Fully Integrated)
Understand-ing Your Audience	I create generic messaging for broad audiences	I consider audience segments but lack deep insights	I develop targeted, personalized strategies using audience insights

Digital and Physical Visibility	I lack a structured visibility strategy	I am active but lack consistency in digital/ physical presence	I maintain strong, consistent visibility across all marketing touchpoints
Impactful Presentations	I struggle to communicate marketing ideas effectively	I present well but don't always engage audiences	I craft compelling, engaging presentations that resonate
Conscious and Ethical Marketing	I see social responsibility as an afterthought	I acknowledge its importance but don't always integrate it	I ensure marketing aligns with ethical, sustainable business practices
Remembering the Hospitality	I focus on selling rather than creating an experience	I see the value of hospitality in marketing but don't always apply it	I use hospitality principles to make every customer interaction special

Reflection Questions:

- Are you segmenting and personalizing your marketing approach?

- How do you ensure your brand remains visible and engaging across channels?
- Are you using hospitality principles to develop marketing that is more personal and meaningful to your customers or guests?

10

Bringing it All Together: The Scorecard in Full

Marketing is not linear nor is it a one-time effort; it's an ongoing cycle of execution, evaluation, and refinement. A productive marketing mindset requires continuous learning, data-driven adjustments, and a commitment to aligning marketing strategies with broader business goals.

This scorecard helps us assess how well we've adapted the principles of this book into our approach. Have we moved beyond execution to optimization? Are we making strategic decisions based on meaningful data? The goal is not just to implement marketing tactics but to refine them over time, so efforts drive immediate results and long-term impact.

As we evaluate ourselves in the areas of data-driven decision-making, holistic ROI evaluation, and marketing accountability, think about how our marketing approaches have evolved.

Measuring Success and Refining Strategy

Milestone: From Execution to Continuous Improvement

Concept	1 (Needs Work)	3 (Getting There)	5 (Fully Integrated)
Data-Driven Decision Making	I don't track marketing effectiveness	I measure results but don't use insights to refine strategy	I continuously analyze data and adjust marketing for better results
Holistic ROI Evaluation	I focus only on short-term financial metrics	I consider brand impact but don't measure it effectively	I assess both tangible and intangible marketing ROI
Marketing Accountability	I struggle to connect marketing to business outcomes	I track impact but lack a structured approach	I measure and report on marketing's contribution to business goals

Reflection Questions:

- Are you consistently measuring marketing performance beyond vanity metrics?
- How do you ensure marketing efforts align with broader business objectives?
- What adjustments have you made based on data insights?

Final Reflection:

- How has your marketing mindset evolved while reading this book?
- What areas do you still need to strengthen?
- How will you apply these principles in your future marketing efforts?

Next Steps:

- Revisit chapters where you scored lower to reinforce learning.
- Continue evolving your marketing mindset beyond the book by engaging with industry trends.
- Apply hospitality-driven marketing principles in all aspects of your work, regardless of industry.

Final Thoughts: A Marketing Mindset in Motion, Inspired by Hospitality

Marketing is a constant evolution, and so is our mindset. That's why we must keep learning, adapting and improving.

Keep your marketing mindset in motion. Stay curious, stay strategic, and above all, bring a hospitality-driven approach to every interaction because making people feel valued isn't just good marketing; it's good business.

Acknowledgments

This book was inspired by my students and the joy I have teaching in a college classroom. Thank you to all the students who sat through my courses—as an adjunct at New York University, as a visiting professor at ESSEC Business School in France, and as full-time faculty at Boston University's School of Hospitality. I learned from each of you.

I particularly love those "lightbulb moments" (as I enthusiastically refer to them), when I see a student "getting it." When they clearly demonstrate a sudden "ah-ha" moment and my lessons click. What is just as rewarding is when a student reaches out, perhaps years after they graduate, and sends a note because something that happened at work reminded them of a lesson we learned together years earlier. I just treasure those instances. As I tried sitting down numerous times to document my thoughts for this personal souvenir of a book, I thought of so many of the students with whom I'm still in touch. Whether it's through social media, interactions in the industry, or an occasional text to share a success or accolade, these amazing humans continue to make me smile. They make me proud. We had such great chemistry in the classroom, and many of the students have become dear friends; we reconnect and talk periodically, and that is emotionally and intrinsically rewarding.

Thank You

I have had the pleasure of working most closely with six students who served as my teaching assistants over the years. They know me so well and they have incredible marketing mindsets as well. Thank you, Elise Borkan Mackin, Kim Kibler, Marut Raval, Lawrence Mannix, Mackenzie Miers, and Paulina Preciat.

Thank you to the former students who replied to my emails so willingly to share their reflections, which are included in this book. Many here are BU graduates; some are ESSEC grads. While it was not possible to include everyone's submission, I truly appreciate your contribution and continued connection. For this book specifically, I wish to thank:

Parker Doyle, Vivian Feinstein-Gough, Maura Feltault, Danielle Galea, Leonie Grundler, Mingjing He, Annie Holcomb, Owen Huzar, Joe Johnson, Raegan Kelly, Kimberly Kibler, Pierre Lego, Amanda Lohnes, Elise Borkan Mackin, Lawrence Mannix, Mackenzie Miers, Richard Peet Hanna, Paulina Preciat, Marut Raval, Ally

Rung, Hoda Sherdy, Namrata Sridhar, Alban Sucrot, Jamie Weber, Micaela Yee, Tianyuan Judy Zhang.

And my industry colleagues who pre-read and shared feedback for this book—thank you. Thank you David Atkins, Karyl Leigh Barnes, JoAnne Borselli, Patti Brown, Florine Cagnat, Laura Davidson, Marco Ferrari, Andrew Freeman, Julie Freeman, Emily Goldfischer, Suzanne Jacob, Jim Joseph, Lorie Juliano, Gary Leopold, Vera Manoukian, Abe Monzon, Todd Philie, Dave Roberts, Amy Silva-Magalhaes, and Peter Yesawich – all of whom took the time to pre-read my pages and collaborate to ensure that relevant information is shared here for your benefit. Sincere thanks and tight hugs to each of you.

I want to again thank the readers of the book that preceded this one, *Developing Your Marketing Mindset: Real-World Lessons from Hospitality*, because their insight and feedback also helped shape *Marketing Mindset in Motion: Real-World Lessons from Hospitality*. Thank you Susie Arnett, Andrea Belfanti, Patti Brown, Brian Hicks, Andy Husbands, Lorie Juliano, Gary Leopold, Vera Manoukian, Chris Mumford, Dr. Jeffrey O, Pete Rosenblum, Rebecca Ruf, Robin Ruiz, Scott Savitt, Amy Silva-Magalhaes, Patti Simpson, and Bashar Wali. Enormous tight hugs to all of you.

I must also extend gratitude to the Boston University School of Hospitality Administration and acknowledge our academic journal, the *Boston Hospitality Review*, for permission to republish excerpts from the Q&As I had assembled in the April and May 2024 *Marketing Innovation* editions. These conversations share insights from professional marketers whom I deeply admire, some of whom are also active members and advocates of HSMAI, the Hospitality Sales and Marketing Association International. For this book, I'd like to shout out a thank you to:

- Julie Freeman of MMGY Global for her highly respected expertise and foresight on the future of public relations.

- Sandra King of the Boston University Questrom School of Business for her commentary about consumer behavior.

- Marc Mazodier of the ESSEC Business School in Cergy, France, for his exceptional accomplishments and the kindness he and his wine connoisseur wife showed me while I was teaching in Paris.

- Pete Rosenblum, founder of Map360, for his ever creative and straightforward insights; Pete and his team do amazing big-ticket activations and work. They are all *wow* moments.

Thank you to JoAnne Borselli and her colleague Scott Madden at Connelly Partners for sharing their beautifully-defined personas that I referenced and paraphrased for this book. Thank you to Connelly Partners's Scott Savitt, my digital marketing professor-partner and a fellow BU alum, for introducing me to JoAnne. Scott and JoAnne, you have been *amazing* supporters of our students, and your knowledge-sharing is treasured. Thank you.

Thank you to my incredible friends in the business who represent the hotels, restaurants, festivals, agencies, food halls, culinary programs, spas, attractions, and hospitality services that have supported and continue to motivate our students in Boston (and in Paris). These opportunities enable us to "peek under the sheets" and see what's really happening. We were able to learn in real time, and many of the projects led to the implementation of the student ideas, letters of recommendation, and even internships and job offers. The students are fortunate to be part of an industry where veterans are eager to share their expertise and encourage the next generation of hospitality and marketing professionals. I'm so honored to facilitate these classroom conversations and moments.

I would like to extend my utmost gratitude to Boston University School of Hospitality alum Charlotte Cook, who enthusiastically read chapters and shared valuable feedback. Charlotte, you are wonderful. And to Zoe Beer, who also dedicated time, passion, and love for marketing to ensure the marketing terms, frameworks, and structures shared in these chapters were easy to understand. Zoe, a very sincere and *loud* thank you.

I am deeply grateful to my alma mater, Boston University, the Boston University School of Hospitality

Administration, and the ESSEC IMHI program in France for the opportunity to share my passion for hospitality and marketing with such inspiring and exceptional students.

I extend my heartfelt gratitude to Dr. Peter C. Yesawich, whose class at Cornell changed the trajectory of my career. His ability to blend psychology, marketing, and storytelling opened my eyes to the power and potential of hospitality marketing. His influence on my professional journey runs deeper than he knows. Years after sitting in his class, I found myself recalling how he would fly from Orlando to Ithaca to teach us—something that quietly stayed with me. When I was later asked if I'd consider teaching in Boston, I thought, *"If Peter Yesawich could travel from Orlando to Ithaca to inpire me, I can certainly commute from Long Island, New York to Boston to inspire others."* He has inspired me in more ways than one, and I remain deeply grateful for his guidance and example. And for the newly-sparked connection we have today.

Thank you to dear friend Andrew Freeman for composing the foreward to this book. I adore you. We have worked together and stayed connected for so many years and I look forward to many, many more. Thank you for your unwavering friendship, laughter and style!

My parents are long gone, yet I think of them (and even talk to them) every day. I thank them for instilling a sense of hard work and ethics in all that I try to accomplish. And I am deeply grateful for my incredible and loving family—Alain, Jordy, Zach, and Jeremy—for whom I work so hard in hopes of making you proud. I love you all so much. And of course, welcome to the family, Kuma. It has been so much fun to be a part of the kookiness and playfulness you have added to our lives. Stop chewing the Oofos! And to the everlasting, immortal Charli, who loyally sat, lay, and begged for food beside me or in the same room as I furiously typed away at these chapters. Charli, I miss you tons.

Resources and References

Introduction: Marketing Frameworks to Shape Strategy

Kotler, P., & Armstrong, G. (2013). *Principles of Marketing* (15th ed.). Pearson Education.

Court, D., Elzinga, D., Mulder, S., & Vetvik, O. J. (2009). The Consumer Decision Journey. *McKinsey Quarterly*. Retrieved from https://www.mckinsey.com

Porter, M. E. (1980). *Competitive Strategy: Techniques for Analyzing Industries and Competitors*. Free Press.

Kotler, P., & Keller, K. L. (2012). *Marketing Management* (14th ed.). Pearson Education.

Johnson, G., Scholes, K., & Whittington, R. (2008). *Exploring Corporate Strategy: Text and Cases* (8th ed.). Pearson Education. (PESTEL)

McCarthy, E. J. (1960). *Basic Marketing: A Managerial Approach.* Homewood, IL: Richard D. Irwin. (Four Ps)

Lauterborn, R. F. (1990). New Marketing Litany: Four Ps Passé; C-Words Take Over. *Advertising Age, 61*(41), 26.

Reichheld, F. F. (2003). The One Number You Need to Grow. *Harvard Business Review, 81*(12), 46–54. (NPS)

Chapter 1: Primary and Secondary Research for Smarter Marketing

Lanz, L. (2024, April). Insights into Marketing: An Interview with Professor Marc Mazodier. *Boston Hospitality Review, Marketing Innovation Edition, Part I.* https://www.bu.edu/bhr

Grayson, L. E., & Sheikholeslami, G. (1994). *Euro Disney or Euro Disaster?* Darden Business Publishing.

Lanz, J., Bagnera, S., & Cheltault, M. (2022, October 18). Extended Stay America: HR Success Amid COVID-19 Pandemic. *Journal of Hospitality & Tourism Cases.*

SiteMinder. (2022, October 18). *Hotel SWOT Analysis: Examples and Template.* SiteMinder. https://www.siteminder.com/r/hotel-swot-analysis/

Semrush. (2024, February 14). *Mobile vs. Desktop Use and Trends in 2024*. Semrush. https://www.semrush.com/blog/mobile-vs-desktop-usage/

Wilson, S. (2021). Where Brands Are Reaching Gen Z. *Harvard Business Review*.

Chapter 2: Speaking and Writing the Language of Marketing

Mida Restaurant. (n.d.). *Mida Restaurant*. https://midarestaurant.com/

Mintel. (n.d.). *Mintel*. https://www.mintel.com/

Clear, J. (2018). *Atomic Habits: An Easy & Proven Way to Build Good Habits & Break Bad Ones.* Avery.

Deshpande, R., & Rohit, K. (2015). *Taj Hotels Resorts and Palaces.* (Rev. ed.). Harvard Business School Publishing.

Gallo, C. (2014). *Talk Like TED: The 9 Public-Speaking Secrets of the World's Top Minds*. St. Martin's Press.

Chapter 4: Know Your Audience: Personas, Positioning, and the Power of a Marketing Mix

Lanz, L. (2024, April). Insights into Marketing: An Interview with Julie Freeman, *Boston Hospitality*

Review, Marketing Innovation Edition, Part I.
https://www.bu.edu/bhr

Lanz, L. (2024, April). Insights into Marketing: An Interview with Sandra King, *Boston Hospitality Review, Marketing Innovation Edition, Part I.* https://www.bu.edu/bhr

Vyshnavi, P. (2023, February 13). *Dove Marketing Strategy: Campaigns that Changed the Brand.* StartupTalky. from https://startuptalky.com/dove-marketing-strategy-campaigns/

Lanz, L. (2024, April). Insights into Marketing: An Interview with Professor Marc Mazodier. *Boston Hospitality Review, Marketing Innovation Edition, Part I.* https://www.bu.edu/bhr

MMGY Global Solutions. (n.d.). *TRiPs: Traveler Audience Segments.* https://solutions.mmgyglobal.com/trips/

Chapter 5: The Power of Physical and Digital Visibility

Batat, W. (2020). *Experiential Marketing: Consumer Behavior, Customer Experience, and the 7Es.* Routledge.

HubSpot. (2024). *How Video Consumption Is Changing in 2024.* Retrieved from https://blog.hubspot.com/marketing/how-video-consumption-is-changing

HubSpot. (2024). *The HubSpot Blog's 2024 Video Marketing Report*. Retrieved from https://blog.hubspot. com/marketing/video-marketing-report

Chaffey, D. (2020). *Digital Marketing: Strategy, Implementation, and Practice* (7th ed.). Pearson Education.

Nwankwo, C. (n.d.). *Customer Sentiment Analysis with AI: Use Cases and AI Solutions*. Insight7.

Team DigitalDefynd. (2025). *10 Ways Coca-Cola is Using AI – Case Study*. DigitalDefynd. https://digitaldefynd. com/IQ/ways-coca-cola-uses-artificial-intelligence/

Digital HEC Montréal. (2023, March 15). *Sephora's AI Beauty Innovations*. Digital HEC Montréal. https:// digital.hec.ca/en/blog/sephoras-ai-beauty-innovations

Head of AI. (2025, February 20). *Netflix's AI Personalization Strategy Saves $1 Billion Yearly in Customer Retention*. https://headofai.ai/ netflixs-ai-personalization-strategy-saves- 1-billion-yearly-in-customer-retention/

HubSpot. (n.d.). *Boost Efficiency with HubSpot Marketing Automation*. Retrieved May 26, 2025, from https://www.hubspot.com/products/marketing/ marketing-automation

Adams, P. (2025, March 19). *How Unilever's AI Marketing Bets are Increasing Production Efficiency*. Marketing Dive. https://www.marketingdive.com/news/unilever-ai-marketing-bets-halve-production-costs-double-speed/742913/

Kumar, V., & Reinartz, W. (2016). Creating Enduring Customer Value. *Journal of Marketing, 80*(6), 1-13.

Smith, A. (2021). How AI is Transforming Marketing. *Harvard Business Review.*

Izzy's San Francisco. (n.d.). *Izzy's San Francisco.* Retrieved January 28, 2025, from https://www.izzyssanfrancisco.com/

Lanz, L. (2018, February 13). *Cutting Through the Online Hospitality Clutter: 10 Best Practices for Organic Visibility*. Boston University. From https://www.bu.edu/bhr/2018/02/13/bhr-f-18-1-lanz-cutting-through-the-online-hospitality-clutter-10-best-practices-for-organic-visibility/

Kim, W. (2024, November 20). *Why do Hotel Lobbies Smell Like That?* Bloomberg. Retrieved from https://www.bloomberg.com/news/articles/2024-11-20/why-do-hotel-lobbies-smell-like-that

Chapter 6: The Power of the Presentation

TED. (n.d.). *TED: Ideas Worth Spreading*. TED. https://www.ted.com/

Gallo, C. (2014). *Talk Like TED: The 9 Public-Speaking Secrets of the World's Top Minds*. St. Martin's Press.

Chapter 7: Conscious Marketing and Impactful Partnerships

Joseph, J. (2020). *The Conscious Marketer: Inspiring a Deeper and More Conscious Brand Experience*. Amplify Publishing Group.

Martinez, V. (2024, May 23). *Ethical Marketing: Building Trust and Consumer Engagement in the Digital Age*.

FutureB2B. https://www.futureb2b.com/resources/ ethical-marketing-building-trust-and-consume r-engagement-in-the-digital-age/

Lanz, L. (2024, May). Insights into Marketing: An Interview with Dylan Huey. *Boston Hospitality Review, Marketing Innovation Edition, Part II*. https://www.bu.edu/bhr

Lanz, L. (2024, May). Insights into Marketing: An Interview with Roger Drake. *Boston Hospitality Review, Marketing Innovation Edition, Part II*. https://www.bu.edu/bhr

Lanz, L. (2024, April). Insights into Marketing:
An Interview with Julie Freeman, *Boston Hospitality
Review, Marketing Innovation Edition, Part I*.
https://www.bu.edu/bhr

International Financial Reporting Standards. (n.d.).
Sustainability Accounting Standards Board (SASB).
https://sasb.ifrs.org/

Global Reporting Initiative. (n.d.). *Global Reporting
Initiative*. https://www.globalreporting.org/

Natura Brasil. (n.d.). *Sustainable Development*.
https://www.naturabrasil.fr/en-us/our-values/
sustainable-development

UNIQLO. (n.d.). *RE.UNIQLO – Giving New Life to
Old Clothes*. https://www.uniqlo.com/jp/en/contents/
sustainability/planet/clothes_recycling/re-uniqlo/

IKEA. (n.d.). *A circular IKEA: Making the Things
We Love Last Longer*. https://www.ikea.com/us/en/
this-is-ikea/sustainable-everyday/a-circular-ikea-m
aking-the-things-we-love-last-longer-pub9750dd90/

Chapter 8: Review the End Goals

Lanz, L. (2024, April). Insights into Marketing:
An Interview with Pete Rosenblum *Boston Hospitality
Review, Marketing Innovation Edition, Part I*.
https://www.bu.edu/bhr

The Economic Times. (2025, January 29). *What Is 'Return on Marketing Investment'?* The Economic Times. https://economictimes. indiatimes.com/industry/services/advertising/ what-is-return-on-marketing-investment/ articleshow/10454642.cms

Chapter 9: Harness the Hospitality

Meyer, D. (2006). *Setting the Table: The Transforming Power of Hospitality in Business.* HarperCollins.

Guidara, W. (2022). *Unreasonable Hospitality: The Remarkable Power of Giving People More than They Expect.* Optimism Press.

Greenleaf, R. K. (1970). *The Servant as Leader.* The Robert K. Greenleaf Center for Servant Leadership.

Boulton, C. (2019). How Apple Stores Cultivate Customer Loyalty. *Forbes.* Retrieved from Forbes Article

Lambert, L. (2021). Tesla's Customer Experience: It's All About You. *Harvard Business Review.* Retrieved from HBR Article

Vainshtein, K. (2020). The Power of Personalization in Luxury Retail. *Retail TouchPoints.* Retrieved from Retail Touch Points Article

Kwortnik, R. J., & Thompson, G. M. (2009). Unifying Service Marketing and Operations with Service Experience Management. *Journal of Service Research, 11*(4), 389-406. https://doi.org/10.1177/1094670509339893

Kwortnik, R. J. (2003). Unifying Service Marketing and Operations with Service Experience Management. *Journal of Service Research, 11*(4), 389-406. https://doi.org/10.1177/1094670509339893

Branson, R. (2013). *The Virgin Way: Everything I Know About Leadership*. Penguin Books.

Angelou, M. (1996). *Phenomenal Woman: Four Poems Celebrating Women*. Random House.

eHotelier. (2025, July 23). *The Evolving Art of Experiential Dining in Hospitality: Crafting Connection Through Cuisine*. eHotelier Insights. https://insights.ehotelier.com/insights/2025/07/23/the-evolving-art-of-experiential-dinin g-in-hospitality-crafting-connection-through-cuisine/

Endnotes

[1] Review sites are a common example of *earned media*. This refers to publicity a brand gains organically, without paying for it, such as customer reviews, word of mouth, or media coverage.

Owned media includes channels a brand controls directly, like its website, blog, or social media profiles. *Paid media* involves paying for advertising or promotions, such as sponsored posts, display ads, or paid search campaigns.

Together, these media types—owned, earned and paid—form the core of a brand's marketing presence and strategy.

[2] If we fail to align our marketing with service delivery, we risk damaging our reputation. It's essential to market in a way that accurately reflects what our operation can deliver. Our marketing should neither under promise nor overpromise the overall experience; we must find the right balance.

[3] Several years ago, I repeatedly used the term "millennial mindset" in the classroom. What did I mean by that? For me, a "millennial mindset" referred to a youthful, forward-thinking approach to life that prioritizes adaptability, curiosity, and connection. It is characterized by an

openness to new ideas, a focus on experiences over material possessions, comfort with digital technology, and an emphasis on authenticity, values, and purpose. People with this mindset embrace innovation, prioritize life-work balance (notice I wrote "life" first), and seek meaning in their personal and professional pursuits. I often thought of myself as a boomer, on the cusp of Gen X, with a millennial mindset.

4   I want to remind everyone: When we suggest changes should be made to a website, we still must get people to the website. Simply building a website doesn't guarantee visitors. Attracting people to the site requires proactive marketing efforts. Likewise, it's crucial to ensure the website is ready and optimized before driving traffic to it.

(This is much like preparing a polished resume and LinkedIn profile before seeking job opportunities. I tell our students, if you share your resume, indicate your LinkedIn URL in your contact details. Employers will look at your LinkedIn as part of their due diligence research about you, which also means that before your resume is shared, have your LinkedIn page optimized first. By encouraging resume readers to visit your LinkedIn profile, you are indicating your profile is ready for their viewing.)

5   Digital campfires is a term used in the *Harvard Business Review* case study "Where Brands are Reaching Gen Z" by Sara Wilson. In this article, Wilson shares the "phenomenon of how younger audiences (born after 1997) are leaving many public-facing social platforms and flocking to more intimate online destinations," which she refers to as "digital campfires."

6   As a side note, the photo shoot of our hotel associates—doormen, room service attendants, housekeeping staff,

front desk staff, concierges, and managers in various departments—to create the imagery on the scaffolding for the two-year project was another wonderful tool for employee engagement and to communicate the nuances of our renovation. A "casting call" was scheduled and numerous staff "auditioned" to have their photos grace the buildings in midtown Manhattan.

There's one more memory I'd like to share about the coordination and preparation for large-scale photo shoots. When I hired a photographer to take pictures of the Sheraton New York Hotel on the day that the hotel's previous signage was removed and replaced, I asked the photographer, John was his name, to work from the roof of the Sheraton Manhattan, which was located diagonally across the street on 7th Avenue. He took fabulous photos of the old marquis signage as it was removed—a great image to share and let the world know the hotel was changing its name. But at street level in the photo was a Marriott Host catering truck. Can you imagine? The name Marriott was clearly visible in my Sheraton photo. Photoshop was used, but at the time, it was a bad faux pas. Interestingly, today I'm realizing it was prophetic, since Sheraton is now owned by Marriott.

7 This reiterates my periodic reminder to students: The four Ps of marketing—product, price, place, promotion—refer to marketing from the perspective of the product. I would like us to look at our marketing challenges from the perspective of the four Cs approach—customer solution, cost, convenience, and communication. We don't want to just market any "product." We want to communicate how our service or business provides a solution for the customer's needs and desires. We become part of their lifestyle. We become their relied upon solution.

8   The terms emic and etic are concepts from anthropology.

> 1. Emic: This perspective is insider-focused, meaning it captures how individuals within a culture or social group view their own experiences, beliefs, and behaviors. It's subjective and rooted in personal, cultural, or community-specific insights. In marketing, adopting an emic approach means understanding and valuing the customer's internal view and personal experiences.
> 2. Etic: The etic perspective is outsider-focused, aiming to interpret experiences from an objective, external viewpoint. It looks at universal or comparative patterns across cultures, often highlighting things an insider may overlook. In marketing, this approach offers a more analytical perspective, allowing brands to draw broader insights and identify cross-cultural patterns.

9   Interestingly, I had spearheaded the Monet in the 90s exhibit for the lodging and restaurant members of the Greater Boston Convention & Visitors Bureau in 1989. Another Monet exhibit returned to the Museum of Fine Arts in the spring of 2021 because it had been planned and pre-scheduled so far in advance. Could this Monet exhibit become a focal point for online experiences to "bring Boston to tourists" when tourists were not able to travel outside their travel corridor? Claude Monet to the rescue again for engaging with Boston visitors.

About the Author

My path in hospitality began in high school with a summer internship on the hospitality training team for Beefsteak Charlie's. Does anyone remember the all-you-can-eat salad bar and the all-you-can-drink sodas? At the time, it was simply a summer job. I never realized it was the beginning of a career in this  field. In college, my "work-study" job kept me in restaurants, where I was a server, busser, hostess, and occasional expeditor in the kitchen. Again, this job helped pay for tuition, but I never realized at the time that it would serve as the foundation for what was to come.

It was also during college that one pivotal course shifted my path from aspiring to a career in broadcast journalism to discovering the field of hospitality marketing. That realization shifted my direction and opened the door to a lifelong career in the industry. (Thank you, Professor Peter Yesawich.)

During graduate school, I held two internships simultaneously: one with the newly-opened Four Seasons Hotel on the Boston Common and the other with the city's destination marketing agency (the latter thanks to a successful grad school class project). Those experiences shaped my understanding of hospitality and the power of relationships. Years later, former executives from the Four Seasons, now with Sheraton Hotels, called me with an opportunity I couldn't refuse: a move from Boston to New York City, where I took on marketing and branding challenges I never could have imagined.

Leading public relations efforts for the re-naming, rebranding, and repositioning of the ITT Sheraton Hotels of New York (and Atlantic City) was an incredible learning experience. Through daily collaboration with sales and operations colleagues, managing crisis situations, and occasional engagements with VIPs and celebrities, I gained insight into the nuances of marketing communication and the importance of working "on property."

After nearly a decade in New York, I spent 15 years at hospitality consulting giant HVS as the Global Director of Marketing & Communications. For 14 of those years, I wore two hats: spearheading HVS's Marketing Communications service in the Americas and the

Caribbean, managing the branding, internal and external communications, and conference marketing of HVS, while also advising hotel owners and hospitality service clients. I later launched LHL Communications, helping hotels, restaurants, and tourism organizations sharpen their marketing strategies, plans, and communications initiatives.

Perhaps the "happiest accident" of my career has been teaching. What started as a temporary stint at Boston University's School of Hospitality Administration has turned into long-term joy, proving that unexpected turns can lead to fabulous new destinations. As an Associate Professor of the Practice, I develop and teach courses in Experiential Marketing and Digital Marketing Strategies. Working with students eager to shape the future of hospitality is inspiring and motivating. I've developed a reputation for "tough love" in the classroom, setting high expectations while nurturing their growth and success.

The lessons we learned in the classroom inspired my debut book, *Developing Your Marketing Mindset: Real-World Lessons from Hospitality* (Hospitality Strategies Press, 2025). *Marketing Mindset in Motion: Inspired by Hospitality* is the companion volume and builds on the success of the first book with practical applications, real-world examples, and technical approaches to help readers "think like a marketer."

I strive to give back to the industry that has given me so much; I am a founding board member of the non-profit

Center for Responsible Hospitality and a member of the International Society of Hospitality Consultants and the Hospitality Sales & Marketing Association International. I've been honored to serve on HSMAI's Americas Advisory Board and recognized as one of the Top 100 Powerful Leaders in Hospitality and one of the Top Influential Hospitality Educators in 2022, 2023, and 2024 by the International Hospitality Institute.

Beyond work, I enjoy spring, summer, and fall mornings at the beach with a good book in hand. Nonfiction enables me to learn people's stories; fiction set in Paris (where I've been blessed with two brief teaching stints) transports me; and food or travel writing lifts my spirit. I treasure Long Island's East End beaches, food tours around the world, and collecting gems and shells. I'm also a passionate advocate for sustainable tourism, koala conservation, and enjoying long walks with friends, especially by the ocean.

Most of all, I am grateful for my husband Alain, my children Jordana, Zachary, and Jeremy, and my dear friends, students, and industry colleagues. I cherish the relationships, mentorship, and inspiration they all share. I am also deeply thankful to the global community of hospitality, because the people I am surrounded by and connected with are among the most giving, supportive, collaborative, and wonderfully spirited individuals one could hope to encounter. It is a privilege to be part of such a remarkable, global industry family.